KIDS SOLD SEPARATELY

FINDING HOME AFTER BEING SOLD BY OUR BIOLOGICAL PARENTS

MIKE RYHERD

Five Stones Press

DEDICATION

Mom and Dad, in a lineup of eight billion, Kevin and I (and our kids) would choose you every time… and we wouldn't trade you for a thousand puppies.

Jesus, You are the hero of my story. You were the hero for every broken, sinful, and rejected person, in every story in my Bible that I read growing up… and I'm thankful You are in the middle of my story.
You got this.

CONTENTS

FOREWORD

LARRY TITUS

Autobiographies are my favorite book genre. I love true-life
stories. But Mike Ryherd's book, Kids Sold Separately, nearly
defies description. It is riveting. My mind cannot comprehend
a parent who would willingly sell his child. Selling up to as
many as 12 children? Ranging in price from as low as $600 for
Mike and his brother, with subsequent siblings sold for more,
Mike and Kevin Ryherd were living like animals and then sold
out of abject poverty by their father.

The story is virtually unbelievable, but Mike's writing brings
home the raw reality. How do kids, even as grown adults, live
through the trauma of knowing you weren't wanted, and the life
you thought you had, wasn't the real story? After decades of not
knowing, now they know. Or do they? Or do they want to?

As the story unfolds, his life implodes. And so does his
family. But when God entered the picture, everything changed.

The Hound of Heaven and relentless love of God more than rescued him.

While reading this story, I wanted to cry, scream, rejoice, applaud, emote and demand justice all at the same time. This is one of those few books I couldn't put down.

The current-day Mike is a theologian, author, composer, musician, pastor and teacher. Not bad for a kid who, like Joseph in the Old Testament, was sold, not by his brothers, but by his parents. How do you deal with that? It wasn't easy.

As you read, you will draw many life lessons and be convinced that with God, nothing is impossible.

Larry Titus, President
Kingdom Global Ministries

INTRODUCTION

"I'm a mess and you're a mess. But something in God's heart loves people who are in messes."

–Larry Titus

Now, let's walk this dog...

*All references to "Mom and Dad" are to my adoptive parents... Reverend Ellis and Helen Ryherd.

** Jimmy and Vickie Hunter are my biological parents... never referred to as "Mom and Dad."

1

STRAIGHT OUTTA CHICAGO

By 1971, our mother had reached the age of forty-one, and in her mind, the childbearing window that never seemed to open for her had been permanently walled off.

(September 30, 2010)

"Dad..."

"Michael, I just got off the phone with Kevin. He told me you were contacted by your biological family members," my father calmly responded.

"Yes," I added. *"Her name is Sarah and she's from West Virginia."*

"It's good your mother isn't here as this unfolds. This was **the call** *she feared the most."*

"Dad, you, and Mom have nothing to worry about. Kevin and I love you. You are our parents and always will be. You raised us and have always loved us. But I do have a question. **Did you pay for us?"**

Dad hesitated, and then subtly laughed. I did not expect his laughter. In my estimation, Dad's laugh wasn't a nervous one, but more of an admission that we *are now here*. Like a seasoned captain who'd ostensibly seen rougher waves than these, he was forever the consummate calm amidst every storm we faced as a family. While our mother had a similar disposition in *most* circumstances, at times, she would exhibit the occasional flare for the dramatic. Our father never did. Dad could've been typecast for the role of Atticus Finch in *To Kill a Mockingbird*. His calm complemented both his courage and convictions.

Dad was born in 1928 in Abilene, Texas. I'm a '72 model, straight outta Chicago, Illinois. Separated by forty-four years, the greatest formations I witnessed of who our father was as a man didn't really begin until I was older, and he'd already turned fifty. My earliest impressions of my dad, within these formative years, was that he was safe and that my brother and I were dearly loved… and *chosen*. Immediately upon *adopting* us, before we knew what "chosen" meant, our parents had agreed to tell my brother (Kevin) and me that they chose us. As they would put it, "*Other parents were stuck with their kids, we chose you two*." Affectionately, Dad collectively referred to Kevin and me as "the bums." Individually, he'd refer to either of us as a "tamale."

I love my adoptive parents equally, but Dad was my hero. Born in the shadow of the Great Depression and having picked cotton across the great State of Texas in his formative years (all the while bedding on dirt floors each night) and having witnessed his father be abusive towards his own mother, something which eventually led to the dissolution of that marriage, he made our home into the Christian version of Mayberry. As a four-year-old, I was blessed to be concerned with nothing more than four-year-old issues. As a ten-year-old… ten-year-old issues. *What do I mean?* Simply that our home afforded my brother and me with the stability and security that few of my friends' home environments afforded them. Our home was stable.

Speaking of my hero, unforgettable among days was one afternoon in the spring of '78 when Kent de Cooke and his older brother nearly hit our car with their Jeep on the streets of our hometown, Newton, Iowa. Brakes screeched. Car horns blasted. Without hesitation, my father abruptly exited our car and confronted the de Cooke boys, now inches from their front grill.

(voice somewhat raised) "*Man, you nearly killed my family and me driving like that*."

3

"*Get out of the way, old man, or I'll run you over!*" yelled the elder de Cooke boy.

"*Go ahead and do it, then,*" my father calmly challenged.

The Jeep reversed and drove off.

At this moment in the eyes of his proud sons, our dad loomed larger than life, staring death itself in the face... even raising a taunt! I was simultaneously horrified at the prospect of watching my dad get run over while bursting with pure admiration that he wasn't willing to let fear keep him from confronting this situation. However, for me, this was a twofer. Kent de Cooke was *my* archnemesis, my own personal bully on the playground. I was a first grader, and he was a sixth grader.

Months earlier, having learned Kent hated to be referred to as "Flea," I put this newfound knowledge to the test and remember him smashing multiple cinder blocks in front of me because I'd repeatedly called him "*Flea de Cooke!*"... from the safety of my front door. Sure, I wasn't innocent, but Kent was fixated on cinder-blocking my face, and this matter between "Flea" and me wasn't resolving itself. Standing taller than ever that day, between me and my greatest fear, stood my father.

I often witnessed my father's calm while my grandparents (who spent winters with us in Newton, Iowa) would lose their tempers and argue wildly. These were the formative events in which, as young boys, we were introduced to phrases such as "son of a bitch" and the especially useful "dirty c*cksucker" (Grandma's personal favorite), and then subsequently introduced to the taste of soap generously provided by Mom after we would parrot the same. *Jerry Springer* had nothing on

4

these events. In the midst of it all, Dad was the arbiter and peacemaker.

Once, in a courtroom in Waterloo, Iowa, after having been advised by one attorney that we would lose our case decidedly if he (Dad) remained my legal representative (which he was) regarding an automobile accident I was involved in... Dad's poise and polish saved the day. We won the case unanimously. The judge repeatedly asked which firm my dad represented because of his demeanor and legal prudence. My father was a preacher.

My parents met in Los Angeles, California, in 1948 at L.I.F.E. Bible College. They married in October of 1950. Their upbringings were worlds apart. Dad's father (Douglas) was a Texas cotton picker who was born in 1884. Due to his capricious temperament, Douglas would lose other jobs in between cotton-picking expeditions across Texas. My father was the fifth of seven kids who were all familiar with sleeping on dirt floors, sharing clothes and living the dream of being cotton pickers across the great state of Texas in the thirties and forties.

My (adoptive) mother, Helen Marie Shawchuck, was born in 1930 on a farm south of Heil, North Dakota. Her parents, Alex, and Ava Shawchuck farmed several thousand acres where she helped with chickens and household chores. She was the second of four kids, the oldest of whom died in infancy. Oftentimes, our mother would remind Kevin and me of what a good girl she was for her parents, in hopes of us exhibiting similar qualities for her and Dad. What made matters worse was that her parents, our Grandpa and Grandma Shawchuck, would tell us boys that she was near perfect as their daughter. *Unattainable virtue.* Kevin and I were hoping (and often reaching) for a much lower bar. While times were easier for my mom's family, both Mom and Dad were born amidst the Great Depression.

Tough times break weak individuals, and, like a hammer and anvil to a good sword, fashion the strong ones. While there are a few preachers out there with mansions and private jets, such affluence among ministers is the rare exception rather than the rule… I know now from experience. As a family in the 1970s, our family of four skirted the socioeconomic line between lower middle class and upper lower class. Most of our homes were parsonages, and I often contemplated, especially in my high school years, where my parents would live when my dad retired. I trusted God would reward them for those years of faithfulness, and He eventually did. Grandpa and Grandma Shawchuck bequeathed their home in North Dakota to my parents in 1990.

While my parents had God, each other and their extended family and church family, my (adoptive) mother was barren. By 1971, our mother had reached the age of forty-one, and in her mind, the childbearing window that never seemed to open for her had been permanently walled off. According to our dad and our extended family, she never complained or got angry with God, she just reckoned her becoming a mom wasn't the Lord's will. *She reckoned wrong.*

At an otherwise mundane evening prayer meeting in Rockford, Illinois, in 1972, my mother would recall being stopped by one of the women who was a regular attendee. She approached my mom during prayer and told her that within a year, she would have a baby. My mom said she laughed out loud and considered that, while well-intentioned, this woman may have heard the Lord speak about someone else getting pregnant, but the prophecy certainly wasn't about her specifically. Our mom always exhibited faith, but in the matter of having a baby at forty-one years of age, she did not. The woman didn't budge or recant but assured my mom that she'd heard correctly and needed to prepare.

2

$600 GOING ONCE, TWICE... SOLD!

How do you price-assess two sick babies? There is no Kelly's Blue Book of Babies, so that day, everyone was spitballing.

My brother Kevin and I were born in 1971 and 1972, respectively. Our biological parents, Jimmy Hunter, and Vickie Sumners, who we will discuss later in some detail, were living around Chicago, Illinois, where Jimmy worked for the Aragon Arms Hotel in downtown Chicago as the maintenance man. Prior to moving into the Aragon, Jimmy and Vickie spent months, if not longer, living out of their van. My brother Kevin is believed to have been born in this van. *Cue Chris Farley.*

Upon Jimmy's getting hired by the hotel, he moved himself, Vickie, and Kevin into one of the rooms as part of his compensation. It was during this time that I was born to Jimmy and Vickie at Northwestern Hospital in Chicago. While preferable to living in a van, our living conditions at the hotel were still such that the State of Illinois had been notified of severe neglect and abuse. Vickie suffered from mental illness and was reportedly depressed and despondent, leaving most of the care of two sickly infants to Jimmy, who was singularly providing maintenance to this large facility.

When my adoptive parents (Ellis and Helen) first received the call from a longtime friend who was part of an inner-city foster care program in Chicago, the situation was critical. What was described on that phone call was later verified by our parents. Babies with bite marks, cigarette burns and life-threatening fever. My dad would often recall that he found Kevin and me eating dog food out of the dog's bowl out of sheer hunger. Vickie, our birth mother, was mentally and maternally checked out.

Our skin was raw from the diaper rash and my adoptive parents, during one visit, immediately took us to their family doctor to verify if we had a reasonable chance of survival should they choose to keep us. Their greatest concern for me (between five to six months old) was excessive water on the brain.

Welcoming a healthy baby into one's life is a monumental decision. Parents in their forties welcoming two infants with severe health conditions into their household is heroic. I believe my mother needed to hear that prophecy (now a year earlier) to even consider what she was now being asked to contemplate.

Even so, she felt inadequately prepared to take two babies, so talks opened between her and her sister Jacque, about splitting Kevin and me up between families; my aunt and uncle would take one boy (me) and my brother Kevin was to remain with our parents. My mom would later tell me she felt I was too young, while she was too old, and she was very concerned they would lose me. Her sister, she reckoned, was younger and would fare better with me. My brother and I grew up hearing about how we were nearly separated, but ultimately, God spoke to our mother once again, *this time directly.*

Every summer my parents would spend two to three weeks in Wisconsin at our church denomination's (International Church of the Foursquare Gospel) summer camp near the Wisconsin Dells where Dad had oversight of the Candy Cabin… *jackpot for two little boys!* For Kevin and me, summer camp in Wisconsin represented swimming, games, friends we loved seeing, as well as our earliest experiences feeling God's presence in a tangible and transformative way… yes, even as young kids.

At age five, I remember worshiping Jesus to the song *I Exalt Thee* and feeling overcome with love for God and God's love for me. To this day, it is my favorite worship song. It was there God spoke directly to our mom in prayer, and she felt He'd told her not to separate us, but to welcome both of us into our new family. Across the next decade, my brother and I would create some of our greatest childhood memories at this camp... all made possible by the year prior to us even being there, *when God spoke to Mom.* Whenever our parents would share the memory of this determinative moment for our mom at summer camp, without fail, tears fell.

Prior to our adoption, on at least two occasions, Jimmy (bio father) had let my parents keep my brother Kevin and me, upon the pledge my (adoptive) dad would return us, after the allotted time together. This proved consequential, as babies tend to respond to love... we responded and started improving with each hug and kiss. In fact, *we bonded.* Through the years, our dad would often reminisce about the day he was scheduled to pick us boys up from the hotel in Chicago for a weekend visit where he found us with Vickie, who was startled that anyone was coming to *take her babies from her.*

She demanded that our dad leave immediately, citing that we were *her babies* and she'd never give us up. We were burning up with fever and battling pneumonia, so, according to our dad, Vickie had placed portable fans blowing on us to keep our temperatures lower. Dad recalled finding us, not in bed, but eating at the dog's bowl, as our bottles were curdled with sour milk. Our dire conditions prompted my dad to search the hotel high and low for Jimmy. Upon finding him, he made Jimmy pledge that he would indeed give us to him and my mom, even arranging for us to become theirs permanently. *It worked.*

Jimmy had a way with women. He purportedly sired thirty-four kids (twelve with Vickie), and even had a daughter born in Holland after serving in WWII. He was better at making babies than taking care of babies, which ultimately led him to make what I believe to be one of the most consequential decisions of Kevin's and my life. He arranged with my dad for my brother and me to be adopted... *with strings.*

Ever the opportunist (as Kevin and I would learn decades later), our bio father, Jimmy, would squeeze lemonade out of any sour situation he found himself in. Always looking for the easiest dollar and the next opportunity, what Jimmy lacked in education he compensated for with outlaw ingenuity. Legend has it that he would annually scheme with a bartender in southern Ohio to rig a local charity raffle they'd both split the money from. Our biological mother, Vickie, decades younger than him, came from wealth in Alabama.

She proved to be a fountain of lemonade for Jimmy. Vickie was not only her high school's homecoming queen, but she was also young and naive. Her intellectual aptitude (140 IQ) was blunted by her mental health issues. Her clinical diagnosis was paranoid schizophrenia. Whether intentionally starting a business or not, Jimmy Hunter stumbled into what became a business plan... maybe his first.

That day in the Aragon Arms Hotel, Jimmy sought a quid pro quo. Jimmy had two babies Ellis and Helen Ryherd wanted. The question for Jimmy: *How much?* The question was not, *"How much did they want us?"* but rather, *"How much would they give Jimmy in exchange for us?"*

On the phone that September night in 2010, when my dad

laughed after I had asked him directly about a monetary transaction to move the adoption forward, my guess is he laughed internally, if not out loud, when Jimmy first proffered this request in the hotel that day. How do you price-assess two sick babies?

There is no *Kelly's Blue Book of Babies*, so that day, everyone was spit balling. One way or another, the State of Illinois was going to remove my brother and me from Jimmy and Vickie's *care*, and one way or another, Jimmy was going to get the best deal possible.

(an uncharacteristic laugh from my eighty-two-year-old dad signaled the affirmative)

"How much, Dad?" I pressed.

"I don't really remember, Michael. Maybe $600," Dad responded.

(there was a brief pause)

"Dad, you got a great deal!" I added to lighten things up.

Our (adoptive) dad died in February of 2019. For nearly a decade, based on that conversation, my brother Kevin and I would remind our dad what a great deal we were. He could've responded with any of the following responses:

"Michael, you commandeered a senior citizen's '69 Cadillac at our church car wash in Belle Fourche, South Dakota, at age twelve, and subsequently wrecked it in a cop chase."

Or,

"Kevin, you routinely disobeyed our rules about smoking pot in our house."

Or,

"Kevin and Michael, as teenagers, you burned up the engine

on my 1978 Chevrolet when I was unemployed in North Dakota, because of complete negligence, when I told you boys before you left to keep the radiator filled with water."

All these statements would have rung true in our ears, but our (adoptive) father would always remind us that among the choices he and Mom made in this life, adopting us was one of the best. Neither Kevin nor I knew growing up the degree to which this single exchange at a hotel in Chicago would impact our lives… or the degree to which we were ransomed from abject poverty and the abuse that awaited us but for this exchange of $600. *We know now. Kevin and I got a great deal.*

3

THE CALL THAT CHANGED IT ALL

Within the next few moments Sarah arranged, and I accepted, a friend request on Facebook, and for the first time I saw a sister, who I'd never met, who was introducing me to a world that Kevin and I had barely escaped.

(September 2010)

Ensconced upon our sectional couch for the remainder of the evening, with an unsweet iced tea and my laptop computer amidst the backdrop of Bill O'Reilly presenting the latest in current events, I heard the vibration of an incoming call. My call screen was a screenshot of the logo on my black and green Marshall Thundering Herd hat. I chose this hat not because I had attended Marshall, let alone visited West Virginia, but because, through the years, our last name *Ryherd* was at times shortened (as a nickname) to "Herd," and the large *M* in the design worked for me because, unless I'm in trouble and my mother would call out sharply "Norman Michael," I've always been "Mike." *M-HERD* was on that hat, so I bought the hat and made the logo my call screen.

Simultaneous to seeing this image on my phone's screen, the caller ID, while not listing a name, showed the call number, identifying it as coming from Huntington, West Virginia. At this point in life, I knew of no one from Huntington, WV, though I was aware that Marshall University, the university my hat and call screen represented, was located there.

"Hello?" I began.

"Is Mike Ryherd there?" a young woman asked.

"This is Mike," I responded, curious as to the nature of this call.

"This is your sister, Sarah," she stated.

"You want to run that by me again?" I asked with complete disbelief that this was anything like it sounded. Had Kevin set this up as a prank, I wondered.

"I'm your sister, Sarah Serena. I just got off the phone with our brother Kevin."

Our brother? Not on a first date… *citing Kevin as her brother too*? Maybe when we've walked this dog a little further, but I wasn't holding my breath.

However, referencing Kevin immediately lent credibility to this conversation that I had not given it up to this point. *Is this a prank? Might the call be illegitimate? Maybe.* But whoever this was had taken the time to know that Kevin was my brother… and *in these matters*, you really couldn't have a serious conversation about one of us separate from the other. This "sister claim" was legitimizing rapidly.

"Our biological parents are Jimmy and Vickie Hunter," she added.

That statement from Sarah sealed the deal. This call was now *the call* that I knew would open a door, for better or worse, into a part of Kevin's and my past life that we knew so little about. *Are there others? How many? Are they okay? What does a sister look like? Did they stay in the conditions our parents had described finding us in? Are our biological parents alive? Why did Kevin get the call before me?* My mind was racing ahead of every spoken word of Sarah's at this point.

Simultaneous to processing everything else I was hearing (and unwilling to miss a detail) I was internally beside myself with the thought: *We have a baby sister! What does she look like? Where does she live? Are there any others?* Immediately, I began trying to imagine the face that would match her voice. After listening to her poise and articulation, there was no question about her intelligence.

I'm not sure how Kevin fared in his introductory phone call… there were moments in this call where I was speechless, but Sarah was steady and answering questions before I could ask them. Her warmth and genuineness were evidenced throughout the next ninety minutes, and this was reassuring.

Growing up in the home of Ellis and Helen Ryherd, Kevin and I had heard the names *Jimmy and Vickie Hunter* occasionally. It was part of the story my parents never kept from us. Details however, aside from the conditions at the hotel, were sparse. The next few minutes of this call would supply many of the most basic questions I'd always had, and in truth, would provoke many new questions that I'd never explored.

"We've been looking for you," Sarah added.

"We?" I pondered.

My mind was exploding with wonderment while Sarah's words were answering my unspoken questions like gifts unwrapping themselves for a child on Christmas morning. Shell-shocked, I was hanging on to every word. What she said next brought me to complete silence.

"There are twelve of us. Kevin is the first of twelve siblings. You are the second of twelve. I'm the twelfth. Our biological father, Jimmy, sold us. I'm the youngest of their kids. I'm twenty-three."

There was nothing in my professional repertoire, my spiritual foundation, nor anywhere within my entire being that I could summon, granting me any reasonable, cognitive framework for what I'd just heard, let alone a response. There was radio silence for about ninety-seconds, and then a return to the conversation.

"Are you still there?" Sarah patiently inquired, aware of the bomb she'd just dropped.

"Yeah, I'm here," I said, struggling to make sense of what I was learning. Every family loves when there's a new baby added to their ranks. Cards and balloons are sent, cigars are smoked… joy unspeakable, *right?* I felt none of that. When you add ten siblings at once, it has a different effect. It was beyond overwhelming… like learning a football team is coming to dinner in an hour when you'd only prepared for your own crew… and you don't even know them.

"Do you want to see some pictures of us? I'll post some on Facebook," Sarah offered without solicitation.

Within the next few moments Sarah arranged, and I accepted, a friend request on Facebook, and for the first time I saw a sister, who I'd never met, who was introducing me to a world that Kevin and I had barely escaped. She was twenty-three years old at the time of this call in 2010, and I was thirty-seven.

I suspect some questions are universal for adopted kids: *Why was I given away? Am I not worthy of love? What's wrong with me?* Thankfully, Kevin and I never saw ourselves as the victims of a tragic story with an inevitably sad ending. We are not victims; we were blessed the day we were sold. However, the circumstances surrounding our adoption fostered other difficult questions.

When my dad first uttered *$600*, that night on the phone, after Sarah mentioned our having been sold as babies, it complicated an already complex set of circumstances. Both Kevin and I understood, based on everything we learned about our abject living conditions, we wouldn't have likely survived. Adoption made perfect sense.

Assigning a dollar amount created a different set of questions for us: *What if our dad had refused that amount? How high could Jimmy have raised the stakes to get the best deal? $1000? $2500? What was the threshold? Did Vickie know, or was it just Jimmy? What, in Jimmy's mind, justified placing a monetary weight that when placed in the balances of his heart would outweigh us?*

As one of the two kids outweighed in the scales of our biological father's heart by $600, this alone would mentally torture me, apart from the knowledge that God was sovereignly directing every step for Kevin and me, before we could take steps for ourselves.

> For all things are yours, whether Paul or Apollos or Cephas or the world or life or death or the present or the future—all are yours, and you are Christ's, and Christ is God's.
> **1 Corinthians 3:21**
> *(*Notice that Paul never mentions the past.)*

After our adoption into our new home, all things were ours. As two little boys who were adopted into a new life and family, the world was ours, life and death were ours (and we feared neither), the present and the future was now ours... *everything was ours...except the past*. It was now paid off. For a mere $600, our past was gone. The abuse was over.

Curdled milk in our bottles and human bite marks were now

merely reminders of how much we were valued by our real parents…the ones who decided to love us for better or worse… at our worst. Our scars are mere reminders, not shackles to a past that is no longer ours.

Our adoptive mother, Helen Marie (Shawchuck) Ryherd died on March 5, 2002. I was twenty-nine years old. She was diagnosed about six months earlier with abdominal cancer. Mom fought until she couldn't fight anymore… her emaciated body now riddled with cancer. She was suffering, but she never complained once. I learned in her last six months that prayer isn't getting what we want, because we'd prayed like never before for her healing.

Prayer is coming into agreement with God's will… He wants us to pray, but He won't be manipulated to do our will, even in fervent prayer… He wants us to surrender our will to His own. She went into a severe coma during her last three to four days of her life on earth… but she left me with something on her last day that I'll never forget.

Every morning of our growing up, Mom could be found, before or after making us breakfast, sipping coffee, and reading the Psalms… in her recliner in Blakesburg, Iowa… or on her porch swing in Fort Dodge, which she relished. Now, I love reading the Psalms, but not at the expense of never reading the other sixty-five books God inspired… it seemed to me that Mom would read that book every morning at such expense.

During her last week, as she approached the end, our prayers changed from "God, heal Mom" to "God, please take her and end her suffering." She hadn't spoken for days, and no one wants to see their loved ones slowly dying or in pain. The night she died, my Uncle Norman, my Aunt Jacque and I were in our living room, where Mom's hospice bed held her nearly lifeless body. We all knew the end was soon, but it seemed as if nothing had changed, for better or worse, within the last three days... every breath had been a struggle to sustain her.

Relatively certain she was already unable to hear anything being said around her, I opened my Bible to Psalm 37, and proceeded, from the first verse, to read the entire chapter in her presence. I did it to honor her, without expecting any sort of response.

As my Uncle Norman and Aunt Jacque were conversing about who knows what, I made my way to the fourth verse:

> Delight yourself in the Lord and He will give you
> the desires of your heart. Commit your way
> to Him, trust in Him, and He will act.
> **Psalm 37:4–5**

Mom's breathing immediately shifted from shallow breaths into severely labored breaths... so much so that I stopped reading and was about to get up and check on her. My Uncle Norman immediately spoke:

"Michael, keep reading."

I continued but wasn't paying nearly as much attention now to my own voice as to Mom's stressed condition. For the next two hours, her breathing pattern never changed, until she stopped breathing altogether. *My takeaway?* Mom was not only hearing a portion of the Bible so familiar to her... so comforting... that she may well have entered heaven with words that had guided her all along her seventy-one-year path in life.

Those words were the life that remained living within her, while her body was wasting away. And to hear one of her kids reading this Psalm aloud indicated to her that her faith wouldn't die with her but had been passed on as an inheritance to her kids.

Thankfully, our adoptive father lived for another seventeen years after Mom died… even, at seventy-seven, marrying JoAnne Schmidt, one of the members of this church he continued to pastor after Mom's death.

Kevin and I had a heyday with the thought of our father *dating* a woman at the age of seventy-seven. We ruthlessly commenced to place upon him the very expectations he and Mom had placed on the both of us as teenagers.

"Dad, you better not be handling her merchandise…"

"Reverend, don't let us catch you both in the back seat."

"If we find you two horizontal, we'll be very upset."

During our routine interrogations processes, Dad was normally calm and dismissive, but we'd get an occasional,

"Okay, you two… shut up. That's enough."

A few weeks before Dad and Jo tied the knot with roughly one hundred wedding guests in attendance, I hatched the ingenious idea of purchasing hot-pink furry handcuffs for the newlyweds. I had the box neatly wrapped with a bow on top to boot. The card read:

Best Wishes to the Happy Couple…. With Love, from Kevin

My job was simple: make sure *this gift* was one of the first ones opened for all to see. Like clockwork, Dad (*Reverend*

Ryherd to most there that day) read the card, opened the present and raised fuzzy pink handcuffs in front of everyone. You could hear a pin drop… Kevin looked as stunned as everyone else in the room, until he saw me laughing at his expense. He gave me a look of *You got me this time, little brother.*

As he climbed the ladder toward age ninety, Dad slowed way down. Our house in Texas was a two-story home with all four bedrooms upstairs. When Dad visited from North Dakota, I'd move one bed downstairs to our rear living room where he'd sleep and spend most of his time while we were at home. In previous years, he'd make the climb upstairs to the bedroom where he'd stay, but as time passed, climbing stairs was consigned to the past.

However, every member of our family knew that on Sunday morning, the preacher we all knew and loved would get a little skip in his step when it was time to go to church. He would speed up with his walker. Imagine if you will a ninety-year-old going from *really really slow* to just *really slow*. For any other onlookers, this spectacle would've packed a lackluster punch, but to us, it was Dad still being Dad.

"Are we going to church?" he'd ask as his pace quickened. We'd hear from Jo that every Sunday morning in North Dakota, he would get a spring in his step on the way to church. His question was always the same: *"Are we going to church?"* Dad's life was built around the church and his zeal for God's house never left, even when his mobility had. Sunday after Sunday, on his way out of the house and into God's house, the question was the same, *"Are we going to church?"*

Dad and I spoke for roughly eight minutes the night before

he died. I remember telling him I was considering buying a pair of cowboy boots to which he replied, *"Well, you live in Texas, Michael. You ought to have a pair of boots."* I don't remember much else except that he put my cousin, Steve Bauer on the phone. Steve and I conversed for a few minutes, I said my goodbyes to both, and I went to bed. That was the last time we spoke.

I read about my dad's death on social media. Our church had a potluck lunch that day, and I was there until roughly 2 p.m. I'd noticed that Kevin had tried to call, but I got to his post before I got him on the phone. After planning to come to North Dakota on the phone, I called my cousin Steve to have him walk me through that morning, step by step.

Steve was overwhelmed with emotion... but both Kevin and I were grateful Dad wasn't alone in his final hours, but with family. In fact, he was supposed to have an at-home nurse with him that night but insisted that Steve stay with him instead of her. Steve consented and stayed at Dad's house.

As Steve told it, Dad had gotten out of bed before Steve himself had woken up that morning. When Steve got to his room, Dad was putting on a button-down shirt (something he'd needed assistance with for years). When Steve began to help Dad with his buttons, he recalled my dad handing him a comb, suggesting that he'd need to get started with that next. Dad was getting ready to go to church, but that isn't what Dad spoke that morning. When Steve recounted the details to me, conspicuously absent was Dad's favorite question on his way to church, "Are we going to church?" Instead, it went like this:

"Uncle Ellis, why did you pick out such a nice shirt?"

"I always get dressed up to go to my Father's house," Dad responded.

A few minutes later, Dad would be seated in the passenger seat next to Steve, but he'd never make it to church that morning. He hadn't dressed for church this morning, *he'd gotten dressed up to go to his Father's house on February 3, 2019.*

4

DIME A DOZEN

Learning about the damage and dysfunction widely spread across our biological siblings' lives bound up in this story felt like visiting the ruins of a French village after a German bombing raid in World War II.

"Kevin, you, Loren, Kessler, Bryan, Charles, Dennis, Jennifer, Scott, Christy, Travis and me," Sarah enumerated as if calling the attendance role in an elementary classroom.

Internally I'm pondering the thoughts: *This didn't sound anything like my life… I am from a nuclear family of four. How could it be family instantly? What is the right response to learning I was one of twelve kids sold by our biological parents? What are these people/siblings expecting of me? Why were we the last ones to know? Am I going to have to sit on Oprah's couch to sort this out?*

"We can call Christy and Scott in a few minutes. Would you like to see a picture of our biological mom and dad?" she asked.

Immediately I was conflicted. Meeting and taking some introductory steps with siblings were one thing… a very different emotion surfaced when I was presented with the option of seeing my biological parents for the first time.

"Are they alive?" I inquired.

"Jimmy died in 2006," she explained. *"He had other children outside of those he shared with Vickie… thirty-four altogether. We have a half-sister in Holland who was conceived during one of Jimmy's tours of duty in WWII. She is approximately seventy-one years old."*

Normally, this kind of statement would elicit pure shock… but that shock came earlier in the call and now whatever unfolded was just *par for the course* in a story that only seemed to become more unbelievable and estranged from anything in my own experience.

"Vickie is alive," Sarah shared. *"She lives in a care facility*

not far from where I'm calling you from. We see her from time to time."

Within moments, without ever answering Sarah's question about wanting to see my biological parents via Facebook, at the age of thirty-seven, I was looking at my biological mother for the first time. I was consciously monitoring my emotions. I felt no anger. I felt no bitterness or unforgiveness. In fact, I felt little emotion whatsoever, as if being presented a picture of a distant relative that I'd never met.

The one emotion that I remember being keenly aware of in that moment was how grateful I was for my real (adoptive) parents. Learning about the damage and dysfunction widely spread across the kids'/siblings' lives bound up in this story felt like visiting the ruins of a French village after a German bombing raid in World War II. For the first time in my life, I understood the gravity of Kevin's and my situation, and I felt like we were survivors of something that could've easily destroyed us.

Within moments I was seeing pics of biological sisters, brothers, aunts, uncles, nieces, nephews, and cousins… all of whom we'd never met… and Jimmy Hunter (bio father), seated on concrete steps outside of some obscure building, next to Vickie.

Weird as it may sound, I had no concept of what either of my biological parents would look like, but when I saw Vickie, she looked every bit the part. I could see features in her face that matched Kevin's and my own. Jimmy's appearance, not so much. I was expecting someone bigger.

Both Kevin and I have bigger frames. Jimmy was skinny,

and in this pic of low resolution, had a scruffy gray beard worthy of a drunken sailor who'd seen too many storms, leaving his facial features less distinguishable. To this day, it's the only image I've ever seen of him.

While still surreal, the subsequent phone call that night with my *new* siblings Christy and Scott, following my ninety-ish-minute introductory visit with Sarah, further solidified this newfound reality. Interestingly, when I first saw Sarah in a few pictures, I identified her purely as a baby sister to Kevin and myself, with features resembling us both… but thankfully much prettier than either of us.

However, just minutes later when I began to visit with Christy, and saw pics of her, I immediately saw more resemblance of Sarah to Kevin and Christy to me. Before this phone call, these kinds of thoughts wouldn't have even registered with me, because my view of the world was never biological (for me) prior to these new revelations. That call changed everything.

At the time of this phone call, I was thirty-seven years old. Kevin was thirty-eight. I had lived with Kevin and myself for thirty-seven years. *I knew us.* Despite a few claims to the contrary, I knew neither of us was clinically insane. This may sound a little harsh, but aside from all the wonderment and excitement of meeting new siblings, there were also question marks they had about us, just as we had question marks about them.

Every family has a crazy uncle or aunt, right? Paranoid schizophrenia is hereditary. Considering our genetic pool, in the light of knowing Jimmy's penchant for all things criminal (including selling his own kids), Vickie's clinical diagnosis, and the inhumane *care* and abuse all twelve of us received from our biological parents, you begin to ponder: *who might have snapped? Who might the schizophrenia gene have passed on to? Which of the kids landed in a situation better or worse than Kevin's and mine? How did they adjust to knowing, if their parents told them they were sold, they were given away by the two people who should've loved them the most? What was I opening my own family up to by embracing a new family?*

These questions are ugly but honest, and my intent was never to write a pretty account of this saga, but to give an honest account. There simply isn't enough lipstick for a pig like this.

5

DADDY ISSUES

I would hug them, but not like my female counterparts… no gentle pats or lipsticky smiles… kid after kid, I'd put them in a headlock, and even put a "little mustard on it."

For better or worse, human beings are tribal. This can be a source of great comfort and strength but also a source of great tragedy and consequence. When a family sticks together through the most bitter suffering and loss, we see the tribe at its best. When one lays his or her life down for another, whether for a friend or brother-in-arms, this is the greatest example of love.

Sadly, the opposite is equally true. Ostracizing or belittling someone from a different culture or race, not because of their actions or character, is when the tribe is at its worst. Judgments made that are merely skin-deep fuel genocide… Adolf Hitler being the poster boy.

In America, radicalized groups such as the KKK, BLM and other groups of all political and ethnic stripes foment hatred against those who can do nothing about the skin they were born in.

After that call, new questions were surfacing:

*Who is my tribe now? Will this tribe, to the degree Kevin or I seek acceptance, accept us? Is our acceptance a birthright within the group? What if I'm uncomfortable with them? We are all siblings who were dealt a wild hand, at no fault of our own, but am I required to play this hand or can I momentarily welcome this temporarily, and then quickly return to life as normal? What about Kevin? What does this mean for our relationship now that we have these **others** in our lives? Am I expected to buy Christmas gifts for all my nieces and nephews?*

Tentative arrangements were made that night on the phone with Sarah, Christy, and Scott to get as many of us as possible together in roughly six weeks. Sarah and Christy offered to host everyone at their homes in West Virginia, while other siblings began to make travel plans. Meanwhile… my determination was to keep on trucking… love my family, go to work, pay bills. Hindsight now makes it clear that this was merely wishful thinking on my part.

After finally going to bed that first night, having scoured over every sibling's Facebook pics and information, I attempted to carry on the next morning as usual. In 2010, I was married with three beautiful daughters who were between the ages of nine to thirteen. Between ministry positions, I found myself coaching middle school athletics in Lewisville, Texas, and it was there God opened a new door of ministry, unlike any previous one.

As a former college football player, I assumed that my athletic gifting from earlier years would automatically translate into successfully coaching young athletes in middle school. Nope. I hated it. There were too many different positions on the football field (now as a coach) to keep track of at once. Too many *cause and effect* details between respective positions I'd never bothered to ponder.

I played quarterback on offense and free safety on defense… these two positions were all I knew… and my understanding of the game was too myopic for a coach (even in middle school) to be aware of. I was a player, not a coach. In addition, there were too many hours spent washing nasty middle school boy laundry. Worst of all, there were way too many hours away from my own family at night. Coaches, even at the middle school level, make a great sacrifice. *I see y'all.*

While I may have hated the long hours, long bus rides, etc., the kids loved me. Kids know when you love them and are interested in them, and I excelled at this. The coaching prowess that I didn't possess for each game, I brought individually to the students who were willing to engage with me personally. *How do I know they loved me?* Glad you asked. Here's how…

Teachers and coaches aren't supposed to hug students. This "rule" partly disgusts me because a few bad apples have soured this gesture for everyone else… and kids need safe and appropriate hugs. Physical touch is desperately needed in our world today… especially for young boys who have no father in their homes.

I would hug them, but not like my female counterparts… no gentle pats or lipsticky smiles …kid after kid, I'd put them in a headlock, and even put a "little mustard on it"… and in no time, these kids… all different races and nationalities… were asking me for headlocks. Because this was occurring more and more, a few well-intentioned coaches and teachers reminded me that hugs were "off-limits." Thankfully, I was just putting them all in headlocks.

Before long, I had multiple students, some not even in my classes, asking me for headlocks. They would line up between bells, not for the snack machine or drinking fountain, but for affection. Ultimately, this led to many nights praying on my sidewalk, where God revealed to me a plan after I reminded Him, I knew I couldn't possibly hug every kid who needed it.

As a coach, I took my *work* home with me… these middle schoolers had tragic stories of broken homes where dads were rarely mentioned. Among many of these stories was that of a student who requested to leave class during an exam. The teacher immediately denied the request and asked the student to finish the test before making a phone call she'd requested.

The fifth grader immediately burst into tears explaining that her mom hadn't come home that night… a twelve-year-old dealing with issues too traumatic for any twelve-year-old to be concerned with, let alone math. *She had to make that phone call to know her mom was okay.* You see, Mom was a stripper, and this girl, presented with a math exam, couldn't function knowing that her mom never came home last night.

Math was the last thing on her mind. Hearing this story, I initially subdued my emotions, but internally, my heart broke for this kid. I'd love to tell you that this story was a rare exception. That wasn't the case.

I took these stories to God on my sidewalk in Corinth, Texas. I was already in some trouble for hugging students… kids who were facing much greater troubles. God responded. I'd like to tell you that I always feel God is listening intently to every word in our conversations, but, like anyone who prays, there are many more times where we feel this isn't the case. I know He is always listening, but sometimes the silence on His end seems deafening.

Almost immediately I remember Him giving me the impression that I was supposed to start a mentoring program. *Okay… cool.* The name would be *Hangtime Lunch. He was even giving me details!* What a great name for a program that is simply about time hanging out with a kid in need. *Incredibly cool!* What He said next was not cool. It related to having mentors meet with their students *once a month. Stupid!* Now I began to question if I was hearing from God at all. *Once a month?*

That seemed to be the equivalent of going to the gym once a month... or eating a balanced meal once a month. *Ridiculous.* Now, just to alleviate some of your concerns, I've never audibly heard the voice of God speak. But what I heard next gave me a certainty that I was hearing from God in a way that I hadn't previously in my prayer time. It went something like this:

"If you do it your way (lunch weekly), you will have two to three retired mentors who will join your program. If you do it My way (lunch monthly), you will have an abundance of mentors. Trust Me."

In January of 2011, I started *Hangtime Lunch* at Durham Middle School in Lewisville, Texas. On the student side, I had fifteen black kids and one white kid who were all living without dads in their lives. On the mentor side, I had sixteen mostly middle-aged white guys coming from an affluent suburb in the Dallas area.

How could they possibly relate to these urban kids? Would these kids find any reasonable meaning in sitting across a lunchroom table, in front of their peers, with some older white guy? Was this plan destined to fail?

Scott Siler was a friend who happened to operate a nearby Chick-fil-A store in Lewisville. I remember meeting him one evening, prior to the program's launch, with my desired outcome being that his store would knock $1 off the kid's meal, and the mentors would cover the cost of their meal and their student's meal.

Initially, Scott rejected my idea by saying the at-risk kids I was describing don't need a chicken sandwich, they need dads in their lives, stories of camping trips and a picture of what marriage looks like. In that moment, I remember feeling that Scott was right. *What good is a chicken sandwich when faced with the challenges these kids were facing?* Internally I prayed and God immediately spoke once more to me, so I offered the following rebuttal:

"Scott, they will hear about your camping trip with your kids, and they'll see your marriage every time you open up with them about these things," I countered and then rested my case.

"Mike, if you can get this set up, we'll cover the cost of the kids' meals," Scott offered.

At that moment, I knew Hangtime was blessed and ready for launch. Within four months of the program's kickoff, I received a random call from the Lewisville Independent School District. *Was this the call coming from the higher-ups who'd learned that, in defiance of the rules, I'd been hugging students and had jeopardized this fledgling program?*

"Mike, we've been on your Hangtime website. We love your program, and we are approving it for all sixty-eight schools. We want to make Hangtime the district's mentoring program."

I was simultaneously dumbfounded and ecstatic and concerned and excited and speechless and more. Not to the degree of speechlessness when told only months before I was the second of twelve kids sold by our biological parents, but this was a close second.

"Thank you. I'll get started immediately," I responded.

Hangtime blew up. Within a few months, I found myself speaking in front of superintendents, principals, psychologists, and parents. On multiple occasions, I remember school officials requesting I give their respective campuses immediate attention because of the challenges they were having at their campus that Hangtime mentors would specifically address. They needed mentors yesterday…I needed mentors immediately…and not a few.

Every church was a potential repository of mentors. Every police and fire department had the mentors I desperately needed. I approached them all, and because of God's favor and design, I was soon drafting Hold Harmless Agreements and training mentors. Like my (adoptive) father, I am a preacher…*and I felt woefully inadequate.* Thankfully, when God gives you vision, it is never without provision.

Within a year of launch, Hangtime Lunch had hundreds of mentors meeting monthly, and often, weekly, with their students. Mentors would call me emotionally shaken after their visits, and students were expressing how they always dreamed of sitting at the table designated for parental lunch visits, but never had anyone show up *just for them.*

Up to this point, many of these kids had agonizingly watched other kids whose parents showed up sit at *that table.* This was way beyond anything I'd imagined.

Hangtime expanded into five nearby districts, and I was assigned by the district to make this my full-time role. *What I had lacked in coaching, I excelled at in supplying an even greater need for these boys.* In 2012, Hangtime's model was sent to seventeen chapters of *Big Brothers Big Sisters (BBBS)* across the nation. But for the lack of a technological component,

BBBS even considered Hangtime Lunch for their own national model of acquiring mentors for their at-risk kids.

Hangtime provided a unique answer to a growing problem. Weekly, CEOs and entrepreneurs were sitting across the table from students living in poverty and budget motels…*kids at risk learning the language of success and integrity*…and what marriage and family looked like. Other established mentoring programs were approaching us to make our program their very own. *Why?*

Professionally speaking, I would state it was because of two key ingredients within the design…*unmatched safety* and *unmatched simplicity*. Personally speaking, it's because God is a good Father and cares deeply about the cause of the fatherless. *What I was questioning was God's timing.*

Simultaneously, while Hangtime was taking big steps, I was internally wrestling with everything the last few months had unveiled regarding our adoption. For the most part, I'm an introvert who cherishes my privacy and space, but whose gifting (speaking) has caused me to lead church groups since my early twenties. My emotions got the best of me at times, which was extremely uncomfortable. I couldn't mask my new reality.

The first such occasion occurred the morning after that initial call from Sarah. For months, my preoccupation had been concerning myself with Hangtime and the plight of kids in broken homes. That call… and its timing…shifted me into an uncomfortable recognition of a part of my life that I'd put to bed decades earlier. *I was that kid whose (biological) dad never emotionally attached…and whose own mother was complicit in selling us. I was the kid whose circumstances threatened more than just endless nights of Hot Pockets and pork n beans, but life itself.*

However inadequately prepared I felt in addressing the needs of each of these Hangtime kids, I was even less prepared to face my own broken beginnings. Upon arrival at the middle school the next morning (less than fourteen hours after the call from Sarah) I remember sitting quietly in the coach's office, internally pondering the framework of Kevin's and my first chapter, and thinking my paradigm hadn't merely shifted, but had irreversibly shattered.

One of my dear friends, and a fellow coach, Justin Pipak, asked me how my preparations for Hangtime Lunch were coming along, even mentioning a few of the kids he believed needed the program the most among our athletes. My mind couldn't shift, and I began:

"Coach, my head is spinning."

"What's up? You good?" he inquired.

"I got a call last night from a sister I've never met," I added. As a first attempt to tell him a little about this call, I observed his response and demeanor carefully.

"Holy shit, Coach! Seriously? That's f*cking crazy."

I nodded affirmatively.

"What is her name?"

"Sarah," I replied.

"Wow," he continued. *"Are you going to meet her?"*

"I think so. But that's not all," I offered as I attempted to regulate my emotions. *"She called me and my brother Kevin last night...she explained the circumstances of our adoption in detail."*

Coach Pipak was listening intently to my every word and discerned I couldn't simply or comfortably converse about *this new revelation* like we often did in all our normal daily conversations.

"I learned I'm the second of twelve kids…"

Pipak just sat there blank. No response came at this point, but an even more intent look at me to discern whether this was true…or maybe just to see what emotions I was exhibiting in the light of this new revelation…or if I was just jerking his chain.

Normally, I'm articulate as a speaker, but I was struggling to maintain emotions that were now surfacing, and my inability to continue validated that I wasn't putting him on.

"I'm the second of twelve kids all sold by our biological parents. I also spoke to my sister, Christy, who lives in West Virginia and my brother, Scott, who lives in Nashville. I just saw pictures of my biological parents for the first time."

My was the word I'd just used to describe two sisters and a brother I'd never met…and that was unsettling to my very core. It sounded foreign…even like a betrayal to Kevin ("my" real brother)…and was simply too personal. It was my first unconscious admission that this unfolding saga was a part of *my story* now.

Before that admission in a middle school coach's office in Lewisville, Texas, my emotions were excitement, unbelief, curiosity, etc.…but this wasn't just a story or a phone call I was recounting; "my" was the game-changer. As a speaker I tell stories, but "my" wasn't allowing me to just recount my conversation on the phone from the night before, it was penetrating my conscious and subconscious, and for better or worse, *this story was mine.*

At this point, Coach Pipak was wise enough to not offer any further congratulations or ask any other questions but rose to give me a hug. I haven't forgotten that. I left work soon after, as my world was spinning.

This single conversation epitomized every conversation (regarding that initial call from Sarah) across the next year. Whether I was sharing this account privately with an interested listener or standing in front of a Rotary Club or church gathering, the responses were the same.

When I shared, I'd been contacted by an estranged sister, I was met with congratulatory gestures, smiles, and warmth. However, upon hearing that I was the second of twelve…all of whom were sold by our biological parents…everything immediately became stoic and radio silent. No congratulations…no hugs or warmth…just silence and incredulity.

I keenly and internally felt what they were outwardly unable to express. What they were cognitively and emotionally struggling to process was what I had been cognitively and emotionally processing since that first call.

As a man, I bleed, but my prerogative is to do so quietly and outside anyone else's eyeshot. I resonate with the lyrics of a song: *"I'd rather die than be caught crying, so I'll just smile and turn my hat down low."* After all, I'd been in ministry most of my adult life, and my role was to be the constant among all the variables…just like my dad the preacher.

It was never about *my marriage*, but the couple in my office overwhelmed with irreconcilable differences or adultery. It was never about *my family*, but the single mom whose kids were uncontrollable and considered at-risk. For the first time in my professional life, I was unable to effectively navigate the emotional and deeply personal complexities of the situation in front of me…*my own*.

My therapy, aside from spending time with God and talking to my dad and brother Kevin, was to sit alone and repeatedly watch the 2011 movie *Warrior*, which had uncanny parallels to this story that is now my very own. To this day, and after purchasing at least four copies, it's my favorite movie and it still moves me deeply.

Others have expressed they enjoy this movie…*it's a great movie*…but this story of two estranged brothers allowed me to process many of my own tangled thoughts and emotions. The movie superbly highlights the broken beginnings of two brothers, their fights…and ultimately, their redemption.

6

MEETING MY FAMILY

"Your daddy Jimmy came into our home one day and asked me if I needed anybody 'handled,' like he was some kind of vigilante. He told me if I ever needed somebody killed, he was available for hire…"

(November 2011– Six weeks after the call from Sarah)

"Where are you from?" asked the woman sitting next to my daughter and me.

"Dallas, Texas. It's our first trip to West Virginia," I responded.

"Wonderful! You are going to love it. I grew up there and those are the friendliest people God ever made. What brings you to West Virginia?" she inquired.

"Family," I quipped…strategically omitting any further details so as to not have to explain what I knew would be a long, weird conversation with a stranger on our flight to Nashville.

Ashley, age twelve at the time, is the oldest of my three daughters and was eager (and old enough to manage herself with little supervision) to make the trip with me. I remember advising her that we didn't know "these people," and that I had no idea what to expect.

Again, "these people" are brothers and sisters, *but what rules of nomenclature apply to brothers and sisters you've never met?* Again, the application of the word "my" regarding my biological family (that I'd never met) was challenging in my explanations and often very confusing to listeners.

We met my brother Kevin (who was adopted/sold with me), in Nashville, Tennessee. We threw our luggage in the rental car and wasted no time charting the course for Huntington, West Virginia. Having Kevin with me lessened any feeling of betrayal toward my adoptive family. *Yes, that feeling is a reality in such circumstances.*

Further minimizing any sense we were leaving *our family* for this newfound biological family, we called our (adoptive) dad occasionally to merely stay in touch. Dad seemed genuinely curious as to what our experience would mean to Kevin and me, and probably had some concern as to how it would ultimately affect us both. I'm sure he prayed us through this.

Arriving after dark in Huntington that evening, I recall first being greeted in a dimly lit parking lot by one sibling, Dennis Gandy, from Atmore, Alabama. Greeting Dennis in the moonlight, I remember for the first time in my life seeing someone who resembled me more than my brother Kevin.

He was really welcoming, and I remember thinking his shoulders were some of the broadest shoulders I'd ever seen. I would also tell you he is excessively handsome, but Dennis and I resemble each other more than we resemble anyone else in the "group." Looking at Dennis was like looking in a mirror, and I was hoping not to stare to make him uncomfortable, and probably failing miserably.

Within a few weeks, I uploaded a pic of his and used it as my own profile pic on Facebook. Our sister, Sarah, immediately recognized the sleight of hand/face, but others didn't. In looks, he's my twin.

Moments later, still under the moonlight, I met another brother, Travis Wood, from Nashville, Tennessee. Immediately, I knew he was a brother because he shared facial features with my brother Kevin.

Internally, I remember thinking I had changed. Never in all my previous years would I have evaluated anyone based on biology. Up to this point, it was just Kevin…and blood was never thicker than water because we loved our parents, and they were the only family we knew. Dennis and Travis beckoned us to come inside the church and welcomed us into this new uncharted territory.

In my excitement outside the church with my daughter Ashley, I recall that Kevin had already made his way into the church, and I keenly remember the sense of eagerness to get inside to discover even more siblings, *especially sisters.*

You see, Kevin and I talked about having a baby sister when we were younger, and *VOILA!*...we now had three or four. *Have you ever found a puzzle piece that began to make sense of the greater picture?* Yeah, this experience of meeting each sibling was kind of like that.

Moving into the building, I was greeted by Sarah, and having talked to her and Christy multiple times before embarking on this trip, I felt I had a pretty good idea of what to expect. In the doorway of that church, I was finally face-to-face with a baby sister we'd always hoped for. Sarah was the host/organizer that night, and after a brief greeting and hug, she led us into the fellowship area where I met my brother Bryan Gandy from Birmingham, Alabama. Yes, another Gandy.

Bryan was especially welcoming. He is a conversationalist and wasted no time detailing their own family dynamics. Bryan was the oldest of three biological brothers sold to their parents (both surgeons) in Birmingham. *Did I mention Jimmy may have stumbled into what became a business plan?*

Bryan, and younger brothers Charles and Dennis, were purportedly sold as a three-kid package deal in the late seventies for $45,000. While Kevin and I might otherwise feel very undervalued, having brought Jimmy a meager $600 (that's $300 for Kevin and $300 for me), we knew there was no way Ellis and Helen Ryherd could've landed that kind of financial punch. The price was perfect because we got the best parents two sickly boys could've dreamed of…at a price they could afford.

I would love to tell you that my initial greeting with my sister Christy went great. Sadly, it did not…*at no fault of her own*. Christy Beckett, another beautiful baby sister from Boone County, West Virginia, was inside the fellowship hall and looked as if she was busy with preparations for that night with all the siblings now assembled. Seeing Christy was wild…and I would tell you that Christy is excessively pretty, but she resembles me the most out of any of the girls…so I'm biased right?

So far so good? I didn't initially approach Christy because there was someone else seated near where Christy was hard at work. It was my biological mother, Vickie Sumners. I'm not sure where the miscommunication occurred, but in my excitement to meet and converse with each new sibling, I didn't come prepared to meet Vickie.

Prior to departing on the trip, I'd requested to meet the siblings apart from any encounter with my biological mother, Vickie. Seated next to my other siblings that first night, I sat quietly and did my best to avoid any eye contact with Vickie. Whether this was the right way to go about this or not, I'm still not certain, but in my mind, I had a mother who loved me and wouldn't, in her words, *"…trade you boys for a thousand puppies."*

At one point, Vicky waved at me, and I merely shifted my glance elsewhere. I won't say I didn't harbor some curiosity about who my biological mom was… and what she looked like, but pics would have to suffice. As I explained to others, while I was beyond eager to make the acquaintance of my new brothers and sisters, meeting a biological parent who'd sold us was akin to an Israelite longing to go back into Egypt (where God had rescued them from bondage). This was not bitterness or unforgiveness on my part, just a sense of gratitude that the sale has transpired that day in Chicago…and I was happy to leave it at that. All sales final.

Upon Vickie's departure that evening, my excitement soon returned. Over the course of the next few days, I was catching up on decades lost to the narrative that we all shared. Sarah was an All-State softball pitcher who seriously held her own on the field and off. Christy's and Bryan's wry sense of humor gave me a window into the sense of humor that Kevin and I had always shared but felt was uniquely our own.

Dennis was keenly interested in the dynamics between Kevin and me and was judging that against his own upbringing with two biological brothers and their unique dynamics. The Ryherd boys and the Gandy boys were sold as package deal while the others were all sold separately.

While our socioeconomic upbringings and home lives couldn't have been more diverse at points, we soon found ourselves taking our shoes and socks off at Christy's house where we stayed the third night of the stay in WV. Our feet were all great looking feet. That may sound weird, but they certainly came from the same manufacturer. Most of us had larger than average calves, athletic giftedness and yes, a strong sex drive… compliments of a man who had sired thirty-four of us as if the biblical command to "be fruitful and multiply" was dependent upon himself alone.

A standout moment for me was sitting in Christy's home, which was an idyllic place nestled in a true holler of West Virginia. Growing up, my heart always had, and still longs, for a peaceful place like that to call my own. It's coming, but for now, I'm a preacher who stays on the road much of the time. I'm unclear as to who had the genius idea to play the Johnny Knoxville produced movie, *The Wild and Wonderful Whites of West Virginia*, but there isn't another movie in history that fit the scene like this one.

The documentary features an outlaw family (the Whites) from Boone County, West Virginia, whose stories are the stuff of legend around those parts. Jesco White and his family epitomize the stuff backwoods dreams are made of, and together for the first time with my new siblings sitting together in Boone County, I had a better understanding of the less notorious outlaw, Jimmy Hunter, and his renegade ways.

Jimmy and Jesco were everything Ellis and Helen Ryherd had trained Kevin and me not to be but sitting in that living room…attentively absorbing every detail of this rebel without a cause melodrama on the screen…added a significant piece to this sordid puzzle. It was all coming together with every broken piece.

"You see the bullet holes in the ceiling, Michael?" Gail (Christy's mom) motioned to the ceiling above.

"Yes, ma'am," I responded after locating five to six small holes above my head that would have otherwise gone unnoticed.

"Your daddy Jimmy came into our home one day and asked me if I needed anybody handled, like he was some kind of vigilante. He told me if I ever needed somebody killed, he was

available for hire. I told him, 'Jimmy Hunter, you get out of this house and don't you ever come back.' He whipped out a pistol and fired several shots in this ceiling, and that was the last we ever saw of him."

I offered no immediate response. What I recall was the swift internal rejection of any mention of Jimmy Hunter being my "daddy." As if this story hadn't been compelling enough, little nuggets of gold such as this kept turning up, like French fries in the bottom of a Whataburger sack that only make you wonder if there can possibly be more.

In my mind, Jimmy was the Jack Sparrow of his own little Caribbean. He single-handedly managed to give Ricky Bobby's father in the movie *Talladega Nights* considerable credibility as a father. *Ready for another nugget or surprise French fry or whatever?* When Jimmy had advanced in years and was a permanent resident within a local West Virginia nursing home, my so-called "daddy" purportedly impregnated two females before meeting his Maker. For me, this was and remains the hillbilliest story I've ever heard.

All things must come to an end. When our four days of introduction and intrigue had finally come to an end together, we parted company. Once we'd exchanged our goodbyes and made our pledges to stay in some level of contact with one another, Kevin, Ashley, and I made our departure for Nashville to meet yet another sibling, our brother Scott Phillips (who I spoke to that first night on the phone) and his family as the last stop.

Scott and his wife and two daughters live in the Nashville area and graciously gave us accommodations at their place the next night. Scott was every bit as biological in appearance and mannerisms, and, like Kevin and me, shared a love for football, having played many years himself. Similarly, Scott had a wife and two daughters that were a little younger than my own daughters.

He exemplified many great qualities as a dad and husband, so we had some unique common ground that was established to a much greater degree than that first night we'd spoken on the phone when everything was still so new and overwhelming.

As I write, I've never met my brother Charles Gandy, who lives in Atmore with his beautiful family. We've spoken on the phone a time or two, but as far as meeting, it hasn't happened yet. Another brother, Loren Hamilton, lives in Alton, Missouri. We've never met or spoken. Jennifer Clement, our sister, lives in Waterloo, Alabama, and while we've shared a Zoom call, we've never met personally. I look forward to meeting each of them.

7

A RETURN TO NORMAL?

What the lips of a dad cannot kiss away, requires the embrace of a Father.

I'd love to tell you that I stayed in great communication with every one of my new siblings after that initial visit, but life back in Dallas required my full-time attention in new ways. Besides Hangtime Lunch, which was blowing up, I was a husband and am a dad. At the time (circa 2011–2012), my daughters were thirteen, eleven and ten, and I was running a mentoring program that required long hours and late nights.

I'm forever grateful to a dear friend, Pam Taylor, who excels in administration and problem-solving, for having stepped into the admin role for Hangtime. She got the ball off the line of scrimmage and across the goal line for me many times…Pam was all heart. Others stepped up in various ways. My brother Kevin, a friend and mentor, Sonny Gann, and my best friend, Keith Long, provided wise counsel and were all right beside me.

My ex-wife, Trish, accompanied me to many training sessions and my daughters were more than willing to step up and assist me in any way they could. In fact, many of my daughter Ashley's friends were boys enrolled in Hangtime Lunch.

Perhaps Hangtime gave me an outlet to get away from some of the hidden problems I couldn't seem to fix on the home front. Our marriage was failing, and my ex and I both knew it for over fifteen years of our twenty-four years married, but it was something that we hoped would just work out.

For the most part, I am not a bitter ex, in fact, I don't blame my ex for the subsequent divorcees in 2019; I chose her, and we both brought baggage into our marriage. When we met, we were both young and looking for something in each other that neither of us could provide. I was called to ministry, she was not. She had expectations that I didn't meet as a pastor and father to our girls, and I had expectations I felt she was unconcerned with. She was looking for an opportunity to get out of her own situation at the time.

It just didn't work together. To this day, I've tried to never speak ill of her...just to pray for her. She's a great person, we just weren't great together. Looking back, I realize I didn't pick a bad person, it's just bad that I picked someone who wasn't heading in the same direction. I give her tremendous credit for hanging in there much longer than most spouses who are not called to ministry would've lasted. I wish her all the best.

My kids are my heart. After our divorce, I got an incredible tattoo on my left forearm that has their initials and dates of birth, all with little girl bows to boot. Yes, as a grown man, I rock little-girl bows on my arm for all to see, because there is nothing I've done or achieved in my life that I am prouder of than being their dad.

They too share a part within this narrative of brokenness, separation, and ultimately, redemption. Like me, across the years they privately and silently cried and suffered through this process, but I also know that God doesn't work in *some things* for the good of those who love Him; my girls love Jesus, and Romans 8:28 tells us He "works in all things" for our good. I am more than confident the best is ahead for each of them as they follow God.

At the time of this writing, my oldest daughter, Ashley, who accompanied me on that first trip to meet our newly discovered family, is married. She has an awesome husband, Zac, who works hard and, like Ashley, has a calling on his life for ministry.

Ashley has an anointing in worship and is experienced as a worship leader across many years. When she was just sixteen, I invited her to (vocally) lead our worship services at the church I led in Flower Mound, and she excelled in this role. Her sensitivity to the Holy Spirit allows her to worship extemporaneously and passionately. Ashley embodies tremendous talent and heart…and her voice is prettier to me than any I've ever heard.

My *middlest* daughter, Payton, is my creative genius. At age four, like a paint brush in the hands of Michelangelo, such was duct tape or bottle caps in the hands of my favorite little artist. She was the illustrator in my first (discipleship) book, *52 Lies Every Parent Should Tell Their Kids*, and while she currently assists me in ministry, her own ministry is blossoming.

In 2023, she and I are launching an evangelism project together called "Prisoner Exchange," showcasing her artistic talents. From infancy, this one marched to the beat of her own drum, and she is kind to her very core.

My baby girl, Hailey, is my wildflower. From age four, she was baptized in the Holy Spirit and has unlimited personality and punch. Like her older sisters, she isn't afraid to stand against the tide of cultural pollution but leaves her mark wherever she goes. She is the little one of the three, but she loves big and fights hard. There is certainly ministry ahead of this one, but I know it won't look conventional or predictable. She is fierce.

Any honest accounting of my thoughts as a dad (and ex-husband) provokes within me a certain level of regret. Right or wrong, to admit otherwise wouldn't be truthful, and some of my kids' hurt requires more than Dad (or Mom) kissing it to make it all better. *I wish I'd known earlier what I know now. What if I'd been more disciplined? Why didn't I lead better when I had the opportunity to show them? I wish I could've fixed it all when it broke. And, yes, I wish I would've been a better provider.* If this makes any sense to you at all, then we understand each other. What the lips of a dad cannot kiss away, requires the embrace of a Father.

8

FINDING A FATHER

God is in the business of restoration. He is a consignment
shopper, finding that which is broken and discarded by others,
and He insists on paying full price…

And he said, "There was a man who had two sons. And the younger of them said to his father, 'Father, give me the share of property that is coming to me.' And he divided his property between them. Not many days later, the younger son gathered all he had and took a journey into a far country, and there he squandered his property in reckless living. And when he had spent everything, a severe famine arose in that country, and he began to be in need. So he went and hired himself out to one of the citizens of that country, who sent him into his fields to feed pigs. And he was longing to be fed with the pods that the pigs ate, and no one gave him anything.

"But when he came to himself, he said, 'How many of my father's hired servants have more than enough bread, but I perish here with hunger! I will arise and go to my father, and I will say to him, "Father, I have sinned against heaven and before you. I am no longer worthy to be called your son. Treat me as one of your hired servants."' And he arose and came to his father. But while he was still a long way off, his father saw him and felt compassion, and ran and embraced him and kissed him. And the son said to him, 'Father, I have sinned against heaven and before you. I am no longer worthy to be called your son.' But the father said to his servants, 'Bring quickly the best robe, and put it on him, and put a ring on his hand, and shoes on his feet. And bring the fattened calf and kill it and let us eat and celebrate. For this my son was dead, and is alive again; he was lost, and is found.' And they began to celebrate.

"Now his older son was in the field, and as he came and drew near to the house, he heard music and dancing. And he

*called one of the servants and asked what these things meant.
And he said to him, 'Your brother has come, and your father has
killed the fattened calf, because he has received him back safe
and sound.' But he was angry and refused to go in. His father
came out and entreated him, but he answered his father, 'Look,
these many years I have served you, and I never disobeyed your
command, yet you never gave me a young goat, that I
might celebrate with my friends. But when this son of yours
came, who has devoured your property with prostitutes, you
killed the fattened calf for him!' And he said to him, 'Son, you
are always with me, and all that is mine is yours. It was fitting to
celebrate and be glad, for this your brother was dead, and is
alive; he was lost, and is found.'"*

Luke 15:11–32

If you have no Biblical knowledge whatsoever, and know
nothing else about God, *hang on to this story for dear life.* In the
next chapter or so, I'll walk this dog with you a little further, but
for now, simply keep in mind that everyone in the story had "un-
sonned" the prodigal kid…everyone except Dad.

Upon the younger boy's return, the older brother wasn't
even willing to call his little prodigal brother his own brother
anymore, but merely, *"That son of yours."* The younger brother
had already rehearsed his return speech, declaring, *"I'm no
longer worthy to be called your son."* The father of Luke 15
didn't budge on the matter, but declared upon his wayward
boy's return, *"My son is home!"* God is in the business of

restoration. He is a consignment shopper, finding that which is broken and discarded by others, and He insists on paying full price… *"bring the fattened calf, my robe, my ring."*

God doesn't "un-son" us in our mess, His hope is to always restore us. Like my mentor once said before a convention hall filled with pastors and leaders from nations across the globe, *"I'm a mess. You're a mess. But something in the heart of God loves people who are in a mess."* If that doesn't give you some comfort, there's likely nothing else in this book that will. God loves us and isn't giving up on us when others, including ourselves, have concluded it's over. He isn't budging about us.

As a dad, nothing, Nothing, ABSOLUTELY NOTHING, in my nature reconciles with abandoning my kids. I'm not saying they haven't provoked me a little at times, and at times I've exasperated them, *but orphaned they will never be.* Each one of us brings something of a limp into our relationships, marriages and so forth, and whatever that limp, it impacts our kids.

I'm not saying there isn't healing and redemption from our past failings, but scars often result. When children don't see healthy patterns of communication (especially in resolving conflict), they may well carry those patterns forward. Where there is a lack of repentance from selfishness, unforgiveness or grudges, sexual immorality or neglect, there are often lasting scars. Initially, these scars seem like permanent disqualifiers…*until you run into the arms of a Father.*

In April of 2012, Hangtime Lunch was growing rapidly. Many women were requesting to become mentors, so I approached the participating districts and soon after, Hangtime got in touch with its feminine side. Among one of many opportunities to showcase our program, I was invited to man a booth at a men's conference in Grapevine, Texas. To this day, I do not remember who called to invite me or how they'd even heard of my program…but God's providence was all over it.

I arrived at the convention center knowing no one who would be in attendance, and I knew even less about the speakers or program itself. Upon entrance, I noticed that most of the exhibitors already had their booths set up with colorful banners and the accompanying paraphernalia.

Several tables had books with guy-related topics and T-shirts for sale. One guy even had a sword display. *Me?* I had an empty Chick-fil-A sack and drink as my props, with roughly one hundred Hangtime Lunch business cards. I'm certain there were more than a few folks who assumed I'd found an empty table to quietly eat my lunch.

Prior to the kickoff of the convention, I was making some small talk with folks who'd approached my table, as well as meandering to some others' nearby displays. To my immediate left was a table full of books by the author and speaker, Larry Titus, which meant absolutely nothing to me. I didn't have time to read another book (in my mind), I needed mentors and that was my only objective in being at this convention.

I'm sure you've heard of how people have testified that in the presence of a great charismatic personality, the room changes…the energy shifts…the atmosphere enlarges…and so on. People often spoke of Bill Clinton having this magnetism. Others would cite Kanye West or Donald Trump in such ways.

Within thirty minutes of this convention starting, I had such an encounter.

From no more than forty feet from my perch, I spotted a man on the floor of the convention hall who I noticed carried this dynamism. I was sure the key-note speaker for the convention was in my sights and would be commanding the crowd moments later. To my surprise, he made eye contact with me and approached my shanty of a booth. He could have approached any of the other, better adorned, booths, but he walked right up to mine.

"Mike, I am so proud of you," he said.

"Why?" I remember asking.

"Your wife told me about your program for fatherless boys. It's amazing and I wish I'd have had that in my life when I was younger."

"Really? Why?" I asked the man who I had already pegged as the guy who looked like he had everything going his way.

"Because I spent thirty-five years in a Pennsylvania prison system."

I remember thinking to myself, *"Maybe your math is bad, Mike. This isn't adding up at all. This is the guy. He's not that much older than me... thirty-five years is most of his life. Is he anointed or not?"* Maybe I just don't know how to pick anointed, charismatic people very well, I thought to myself.

"I got out in April," he added, further solidifying my assurance that I'd chosen the wrong guy as *the guy*. This convention was in May of 2012.

"You just got out of thirty-five years of prison?" I asked.

"Just about four weeks ago."

"I'm sorry, I don't understand. You have this presence about you that I saw from across the room. What am I missing?"

"God found me while I was in prison. In fact, I was content to stay there for the rest of my life if that was God's will. My ministry blossomed during my time in prison. I didn't have any clue that God could love someone like me, until God sent Larry Titus into my life."

"The guy with all the books?" I asked as I pointed next to the table beside mine.

"Yeah, do you want to meet him?" he asked.

At that moment I realized I wasn't wrong about my new friend. This guy carried something so great, an anointing so rare, that it allowed him to face prison, even life in prison, with a confidence and faith that suddenly made my own faith feel elementary.

Within the hour, I was subjected to the most unusual and awkward greeting in all my thirty-seven years. Larry was gray haired and about sixty-nine years old at the time. I didn't have time to assess whether he carried what I unmistakably saw on Gene.

It didn't matter now. Everything Gene McGuire told me about Larry, and how Larry became the father he'd never had… never missed his birthdays, spoke greatness over him when most folks would've easily concluded he's probably just another criminal proclaiming his innocence…**I wanted to meet someone who never gave up on someone who'd given up on himself.**

Larry approached me and began with this:

"Mike, you are so awesome and so incredible, and I love you so much." he said with a smile.

There was no, *"Hi, I'm Larry. Are you Mike?"*...none of that.

I remember internally reeling from Larry's opening salvo. Seriously, if anyone approaches you at the grocery store and this is their opening line, I'm doubtful you'd give it much consideration either. You might leave altogether or find another aisle quickly.

Awesome? Incredible? Those were the things my parents said about me, but honestly, I often assumed that was because they were somewhat obligated to say those things because they chose Kevin and me, and they needed a great return on their investment.

I love you so much? You don't even know me. You have no idea how many times I've disappointed myself, my spouse, my kids…I reckoned just as I'd mistakenly picked Gene as *the guy* out of the crowd, this kind older gentleman had picked the wrong one in telling me any of those things.

The boot just didn't fit. *If you knew my struggles in ministry…my self-doubt…and if that's not good enough to imminently disqualify all those accolades, you don't know about my sin… the porn I shamefully comforted myself with because there were holes in my marriage that I couldn't seem to shake.*

I didn't say any of those things out loud and I didn't have to. *Larry knew and he didn't budge.*

"Now, Mike, if you just disagreed with what I said about you, you are disagreeing with the way God feels about you. I agree with Him."

Something shifted in me internally at that moment. Just as Gene's shackles had come off weeks earlier, my own shackles fell to the floor then and there and I assessed almost instantly that I'd been agreeing with everything the devil had told me for decades…lies I'd believed as a Christian…as a pastor…as a man. *Who was this guy?*

Larry had found me whilst in my own private and personal pigpen, and instead of casting me away, reminded me of what my heavenly Father had been trying to say to me for many years. He spoke over me the way Jesus spoke over prostitutes and tax collectors. He spoke the way the father in Luke 15 spoke over his prodigal kid.

Within a week or so, I arranged to sit down at a nearby Cracker Barrel with Larry. After arriving a little late, I wasn't sure what I should be expecting. *Was this new relationship going to be broken in the light of my porn admission?* No. *Would these initial statements be rescinded if I doubted at times?* No. *What about the times I was sure to still fail?*

"Mike, if I disciple you, you will fall…but I'm 100 percent committed to you," Larry offered with a warm smile.

That sealed the deal. I know I'm prone to falling. No pastor or preacher or spiritual leader ever gave me the assurance that *even in my failure*, they'd stay with me. Nothing, ABSOLUTELY NOTHING, Larry could've said was more engaging than that comment. Inwardly, I vowed to stay as close to this man and his fatherly encouragement as I could. *He'd never get rid of me…for my part.* This statement alone meant that when I fall, I don't have someone to run from, but a father to run to. This is discipleship.

Over the course of the next seven to eight months, we'd regularly sit at a local restaurant, and I'd hear from Larry about how anointed I am…how gifted I am…how God was going to use me to reach into multitudes with my story. The more I agreed with what this father in the faith spoke over me, the closer I felt to my heavenly Father and fulfilling His purpose for my life. This is discipleship.

"I'd like for you to be ordained in Orlando later this year."

That October, I flew into Orlando with my adoptive father (Ellis Ryherd), and what awaited me at the convention center was overwhelming. Upon arriving at the conference, over forty nations were represented from across the globe, with their country's respective flags flying high overhead.

Stories of miraculous healings, crowds of people in Muslim nations coming to know Jesus and much more. There was a team of dancers from Australia as well as missionaries from parts of the world whose identities were to be kept private because they risked their very lives to carry the gospel where local authorities would act swiftly to stop them.

I felt myself a little fish in a pond that spanned nations. *Why did Larry take such an interest in me? Everybody is approaching him.* I reckoned Larry must've told them all how incredible and awesome they were, and now they were not willing to let go of him either. Then, Jack Hayford, one of the greatest pastors in the nation, stepped forward that evening and offered this:

"If I've ever met a true prophet of God, it's Larry Titus. If I've ever witnessed a nation change because of the anointing on

one man's life, it's Larry. What happened in Vanuatu is unlike any move of God I've ever witnessed."

WAIT? What happened in Vanuatu? Why didn't my friend who loves pancakes with excessive syrup and who requests two spoons for sharing a single dessert with me tell me this? Why didn't he tell me how God ordained him to be at the Munich Olympics? How the City of Jerusalem, Israel, gave him and his team of one hundred vocalists the keys to the city in an act that was the first of its kind? Why am I learning all the great things secondhand?

As Pastor Hayford spoke, the answer became clear to me, and I realized Larry's interest in me wasn't about his own self-aggrandizing. He never sat me down at a table to bolster his own credentials...*he was there for me.*

My (adoptive) mother used to tell me, *"Michael, let another speak of your greatness, and not your own lips."* Larry had invested himself into helping me see myself as awesome, incredible, and worthy of love. That is how God wants us to see ourselves. This is how fathers speak over their kids.

This anointing is what I spotted on Gene McGuire that day. Gene became *the guy* because, like a good son, he listened to the voice of a father. *Like father, like son...this is true discipleship.*

God's plan for my life was bigger than Jimmy Hunter's $600 plan to *make bank* on a July afternoon in Chicago in '73. God used Ellis and Helen Ryherd to step in and save Kevin and me. God's plan for my life was bigger than my past, and even my present, struggles with sin...and He sent another father just to remind me when I needed rescuing.

To you still reading this account: God's plan for your life is far greater than anything, ANYTHING in your past, and yes, your present struggles included. But...BUT...BIG BUT!...you're going to need a spiritual father or mother constantly speaking identity and life over you to truly believe this. This is the part of the Great Commission that has been long misunderstood, *even hidden*, but I'm going to spend the rest of my life reminding anyone who will listen, because I've never been the same.

9

THE PRINCIPLES OF SONSHIP

Heaven doesn't sit right with God without you and me sitting beside Him.

> All authority in heaven and earth has been given
> to Me. Go and make disciples.
> *Matthew 28:19–20*

The following chapter highlights some of the principles of discipleship that I believe are often overlooked in the church world today, yet they hold the keys to what will become victory after victory when we apply these biblical principles. They truly work…as God promised they would. This list isn't intended to be exhaustive, but a primer for anyone seeking a greater understanding of what Jesus is calling His followers to. If you have no interest in this, you won't hurt my feelings to skip this chapter, because I'll never know anyway.

Rare is the church or ministry that gets intentional about making disciples. It is the half of the Great Commission that is least understood, so by my calculations, we're missing roughly half of it. In Mark 16, Jesus commands His *disciples* to preach the gospel to all nations.

This is vital because the world needs to know Jesus and that He loves people…*people in messes according to the Gospels*…and this commission is to *His disciples*. I want to share with you some principles that I've learned after becoming discipled myself by Larry Titus. This list won't prove exhaustive, but rather, offers some highlights that we often miss outside the discipleship process…even while sitting in church across decades.

That said, here's where I'm asking you to bear with me a little as I suspect I will say some things that will not appear evident, or even true, at first glance. That's because they're hidden. *Don't believe me?* Check this out:

1 - Secrets Are Given ONLY in the Context of Discipleship

That same day Jesus went out of the house and sat beside the sea. And great crowds gathered about him, so that he got into a boat and sat down. And the whole crowd stood on the beach. And he told them many things in parables, saying: "A sower went out to sow. And as he sowed, some seeds fell along the path, and the birds came and devoured them. Other seeds fell on rocky ground, where they did not have much soil, and immediately they sprang up, since they had no depth of soil, but when the sun rose they were scorched. And since they had no root, they withered away. Other seeds fell among thorns, and the thorns grew up and choked them. Other seeds fell on good soil and produced grain, some a hundredfold, some sixty, some thirty. He who has ears, let him hear."

Then the disciples came and said to him, "Why do you speak to them in parables?" And he answered them, "To you it has been given to know the secrets of the kingdom of heaven, but to them it has not been given."

Matthew 13:1–11

Did you catch it...at the very end? "*To you (disciples) it has been given to know the secrets,*" but these secrets are *not given* to listeners in a crowd. To any outsider, those gathered to hear Jesus speak sound pretty *churchy, right?* Similarly, those who gather to hear the Word of God every Sunday at a church appear the same way to those who don't attend such gatherings.

These crowds gathered to hear Jesus, as many do to listen to pastors and preachers any given Sunday, but that is not the qualification to receive understanding of these parables, i.e., *the secrets of the Kingdom of God. The qualification is discipleship.* Sitting in a pew each week doesn't qualify us as disciples...our first step is to be discipled by another out ahead of us.

Where can one even find another to do this? It's far easier to simply preach from a pulpit or stage, but this in and of itself isn't discipleship. Remember, Jesus preached and evangelized crowds, but limited Himself to twelve disciples because this process demands much more time and investment.

When one becomes born again (John 3:3), like a newborn infant, they are dependent on another who is more mature than they, to help raise them to maturity.

> For though by this time you ought to be teachers,
> you need someone to teach you again the
> basic principles of the oracles of God. You
> need milk, not solid food, for everyone who
> lives on milk is unskilled in the word of
> righteousness, since he is a child. But solid
> food is for the mature, for those who have
> their powers of discernment trained by
> constant practice to distinguish good from
> evil.
> **Hebrews 5:11–13**

Discipleship can never really happen from a pulpit to a pew to any significant degree. Discipleship is gritty and involves lots of late nights and dirty diapers. There are pastors who make it a point to shake everyone's hand, and others who will take the occasional phone call. God bless them.

However, a disciple-maker will walk alongside those he or she is discipling and will pick them up and dry them off, and offer some encouragement and correction, when they take their eyes off Jesus in the storm and go under life's waters. This is 100 percent commitment.

This is Jesus' model...to make disciples. Not converts, not church attenders or even Christians...it's not what He asked His disciples to do. He told those He'd discipled (done life with) to go and make more disciples. Since it's His model, I don't even need to be the greatest discipler in the world, I just need to be obedient to His word, which is about making disciples.

Those I currently disciple have come to me across months, and yes, years...often with problems in the same sticky areas... porn, addiction and more. At times, I wonder if they're even trying. It can be discouraging...just like parenting at times. But we don't give up on them, we offer help and correction...with massive amounts of encouragement...until they see themselves as God does, and almost always, if they stay the course, they begin to walk more and more as Jesus walked...even with occasional slips.

Let me tell you about Chris. I met this young man in the deepest and darkest part of my own journey, which I'll detail in the next chapter. He originally came into my discipleship group on Sunday mornings because of an invite by one of our church elders, Bill Bower, and in part, because his girlfriend was attending. No shame about it, he was committed to smoking pot on the daily, amongst other pitfalls.

My encouragement, at least initially, was never to change all his bad habits, but for him to turn his life over to Jesus and trust Him. I advised him that if Jesus was asking him to address any area in his life, then that was between him and Jesus. Week by week, month by month, Chris kept coming to worship services and I kept reminding him that he was absolutely loved, and God wasn't budging about His love for him.

It's been nearly two years since Chris first came to those meetings, many of which I didn't even want to attend myself because of my own broken state, and today he is one of my leaders…and many others have come to faith and discipleship because of Chris's example. About four months ago, Chris approached me after our worship time had concluded, and proudly told me that he was privately celebrating one year pot free. We celebrated with cigars.

Had I recommended Chris just stop smoking pot every day, *who knows…maybe that would have done the trick*, but Chris had heard that sermon before. Babies are far better at taking small steps toward greater ones, rather than taking all the steps at once toward maturity. For those we disciple, first, let's get the training wheels off, then after some bumps and bruises, they'll find themselves much more adept at taking a solo ride through the park.

A baseball player never gets to second base before getting to first base first. A ladder is climbed one rung at a time…we don't instantly arrive at the top…skipping all the necessary rungs. This takes time, and a great sermon will recognize this, rather than discourage this process. It's messy and full of discouragement to the new bicycle rider who feels she will never ride well by herself. It's agonizing to the player who really wants to change the scoreboard but cannot advance from first base to home plate without getting to second and third base in order. *You get the idea.*

Jesus knew it. He didn't merely spit platitudes and commandments for His disciples, and after a few months release them. He was the greatest disciple-maker of all, and He spent three years helping them work things out…with many plunges into the water along the way. This is discipleship.

2 - Christianity Is NOT Merely About Getting to Heaven

According to Scripture, Jesus never once gave an altar call. He invited His followers to take up their cross and follow Him…*while still living on this planet.* He spoke of the kingdom of heaven as a *future reality,* but also stated clearly, *"The kingdom of heaven is at hand"* as a *present reality* we could live in while here on earth.

In fact, *He spoke significantly more about the kingdom of God, which we are to seek first, while here on earth.* If heaven were the end-all, all who believe and are baptized could've been held under the baptismal waters and, *voila!*……we'd get there a lot faster. Maybe we (the Church) have missed (at least some of) the point.

Jesus' gospel always included two crosses and two deaths:

If anyone would come after me, let him deny

himself and take up his cross daily and follow
me. For whoever would save his life will lose
it, but whoever loses his life for my sake will
save it. For what does it profit a man if he
gains the whole world and loses or forfeits
himself? For whoever is ashamed of me and
of my words, of him will the Son of Man be
ashamed when he comes in his glory and the
glory of the Father and of the holy angels.
But I tell you truly, there are some standing
here who will not taste death until they see
the kingdom of God.
Luke 9:23–27

This ain't easy preaching, but it should give us great
encouragement that we are here on purpose. In fact, two of
Jesus' prayers are an eye-opener to this present reality that He is
committed to us being right here, right now, until which time He
comes back and sets up His kingdom:

I do not ask that you take them out of the world,
but that you keep them from the evil one.
John 17:15

And…

Your kingdom come, Your will be done, **on earth**
as it is in heaven.
Matthew 6:10

Let's take a quick look back as far as the very first chapter of Genesis. God didn't wait to complete one chapter before letting us know that He purposed us to be *here*…for His kingdom purposes. Keep in mind, He never makes mistakes, and He hasn't repented about this purpose for His children.

> And God said to them, "Be fruitful and multiply
> and fill the earth and subdue it, and have
> dominion over the fish of the sea and over the
> birds of the heavens and over every living
> thing that moves on the earth."
> **Genesis 1:28**

And…

> The heavens are the Lord's heavens, but the earth
> he has given to the children of man.
> **Psalm 115:16**

If we simply preach that this is about heaven, we'll have robbed listeners of their purpose in the here and now. This gospel is about now and it's time we understand that the kingdom of heaven is at hand.

> The kingdom of the world has become the
> kingdom of our Lord and of His Christ.
> **Revelation 11:15**

We aren't here to merely *get beamed up*, but to walk in

dominion and victory, until this place looks like heaven …"…on earth as it is in heaven." As sons and daughters whose Father has promised us victory, this is the purpose of discipleship.

3 - Sonship Is the Highest Place In the Kingdom.

To my biological father, me and my siblings were a means to a financial end. My own sonship, in Jimmy Hunter's kingdom, was valued at roughly $300. I like to remind my brother Kevin that it's possible that of the $600 given that July day in 1973, perhaps Dad gave $400 for me and $200 for him.

He doesn't buy that theory. Here's what I know to be true: *the value of any object is worth the price paid by the buyer of that object.* Because you and I are of such excessive worth to God, He sent Jesus, abandoning His throne in heaven, to bring many sons and daughters back to Dad.

He left heaven because He valued us more than streets of gold and angelic chorus. Heaven doesn't sit right with God without you and me sitting beside Him. We are His kids, and He delights in us (Zephaniah 3:17).

In the kingdom of God, there isn't a title or office that is higher than that of a son. BTW, the term *son* is gender neutral, so ladies, as daughters of the King, you have no lesser standing. For our purposes, I will use son prolifically, but not to your exclusion.

Why is sonship the highest place? Simply put because sons inherit everything. Sons belong to Dad out of sheer birthright. Sons share Dad's DNA…His image…His nature…His love over us like nothing else in all creation.

Do you every remember seeing a picture of JFK Jr. playing under the Resolute desk in the Oval Office of the White House? (If not, google it now) Walk this dog with me…*Can you imagine if any senator or prime minister or head of state had climbed under that desk?* Let's go further, *imagine any one of those world leaders walking into the president's private quarters at 2 a.m. and throwing up all over his wife, Jacquelyn?*

Anyone attempting this kind of proximity would be quickly apprehended and would never get that close to the president again. *Why?* They don't have the title of *son.* JFK Jr. was the son of the president, and the only one in the room with that kind of allowance. Jr's dad, the President, was surrounded by world leaders, confronting him with issues on a global scale, but Jr had Dad's heart.

When Dad thought of a future beyond the White House (which he sadly didn't get to see), his thoughts rested upon his son …not on those with *lesser titles* like president or prime minister.

In the church world, we tend to think of apostles or prophets or bishops as the highest positionally. We need to unlearn this. Important offices, even titles, are important, but these things are conferred and are often temporary. Sonship is eternal. There wasn't a leader in the Oval Office or any other that President Kennedy considered entrusting his legacy to… *that was the son's inheritance.*

A quick overview of the first eleven chapters of Genesis tells us that everything was about seed. God made the plants after their own kind (seed) and the trees after their own kind (seed) and the animals after their own kind (seed)...and then He said…

> Then God said, "Let us make man in our
> image, after our likeness. And let them have
> dominion over the fish of the sea and over the
> birds of the heavens and over the livestock
> and over all the earth and over every creeping
> thing that creeps on the earth." So God
> created man in his own image, in the image
> of God he created him; male and female he
> created them. And God blessed them. And
> God said to them, "Be fruitful and multiply
> and fill the earth and subdue it and have
> dominion over the fish of the sea and over the
> birds of the heavens and over every living
> thing that moves on the earth."
> ***Genesis 1:26–28***

It sounds like Dad is treating us the way John F. Kennedy treated his son. He has given us access to almost everything because we are of His kind (seed) and made in His image. We are here to have dominion over everything else in God's creation, because He prioritizes us over angels, galaxies, oceans, etc.

Back to seed: from the first chapter of Genesis, we can see that everything was created after its kind (seed), even God's children. By chapter three, we see that the serpent was going to attack the offspring (seed) of the woman. There are even a couple chapters I read through at the speed of a cruise missile… *"so and so begot so and so and seriously outlived his retirement savings"*…yes, those chapters are ALL ABOUT SEED.

Chapter six tells us that the seed was imperiled because the fallen angels (sons of God) had sex with the daughters of man producing giants (Nephilim), i.e., *tainted seed*. That's when we are introduced to Noah (chapter 7), who remained uncorrupted and God sought to destroy all the tainted seed, thus starting again.

Finally, we see that Abraham (Abram) finds favor in God's eyes, and it's through Abraham's son/seed, Isaac, that God intends to bless all nations. God is serious about sons and daughters   ...His offspring.

Let's skip ahead: by the time we get to Exodus, we find that in the very spot where Abraham has been promised his seed/offspring would inherit the Promised Land (Canaan), there were giants (See Numbers 13). *Do you see it?* In the very place where God had promised His kids their inheritance, Satan had set his kids (seed) to steal that inheritance from God's sons.

In fact, the Bible mentions that there were five different races of giants in the land at the time when Joshua led the Israelites across the Jordan River. The battle was between God's seed and Satan's seed for inheritance. *Is it possible that many Christians, as God's sons and daughters, have considered the world as "going to hell in a handbasket," and just want out of here, instead of occupying it as we were commissioned? Perhaps God is still asking us to consider the Goliaths of our time as a fight He's willing to have on our behalf, instead of tucking tail and running?*

Is it possible that the demonic strongholds of our day and age are those God is waiting for us to stand against? Aren't we, as His kids, promised victory?

Consider the following admonishments from Dad:

> I give you [disciples] authority over serpents and
> scorpions, over ALL the power of the enemy;
> nothing will harm you."
> *Luke 10:19*

> Finally, be strong in the Lord and in the strength
> of his might. Put on the whole armor of God,
> that you may be able to stand against the
> schemes of the devil. For we do not wrestle
> against flesh and blood, but against the rulers,
> against the authorities, against the cosmic
> powers over this present darkness, against the
> spiritual forces of evil in the heavenly places.
> *Ephesians 6:10–12*

> The weapons we fight with are not the weapons
> of this world. On the contrary, they have
> divine power to demolish strongholds and to
> demolish arguments. We cast down every
> high and lofty thing exalting itself against the
> knowledge of God, and we take captive every
> thought to make it obedient to Christ."
> *2 Corinthians 10:3–4*

Dad is spoiling for a fight. He's looking for His *Davids* to gather stones. Jesus restored our authority over the entire realm of the demonic and gave us back our authority. I'm reminded of the words of the late E. V. Hill, "*The fight is fixed*"...but fight we must. If we do not demolish the strongholds that the enemy has introduced to our generations, our kids will be demolished.

If we refuse to (using the Word of God) destroy the demonic philosophies and arguments our children hear every day, our kids will be destroyed by them. If we aren't willing to cast down the things that set themselves in opposition to God, our children will be cast down, and our seed will be destroyed. If I'm not mistaken, Jesus told us that we had such authority, that even the gates of hell wouldn't prevail over us. *Maybe He is looking for His kids to fight the good fight while we are here and now, instead of fixating on the nearest exit?*

Finally, in light of what we've just read, consider the following parable of Jesus:

> And he began to speak to them in parables. "A man planted a vineyard and put a fence around it and dug a pit for the winepress and built a tower, and leased it to tenants and went into another country. When the season came, he sent a servant to the tenants to get from them some of the fruit of the vineyard. And they took him and beat him and sent him away empty–handed. Again he sent to them another servant, and they struck him on the head and treated him shamefully.

And he sent another, and him they killed.
And so with many others: some they beat,
and some they killed. He had still one other, **a
beloved son**. Finally he sent him to them,
saying, '**They will respect my son**.' But
those tenants said to one another, '**This is the
heir. Come, let us kill him, and the
inheritance will be ours**.'
Mark 12:1–7 (emphasis mine)

The enemy is counting on us surrendering our inheritance, our generations, and our world to his purposes. *How will he accomplish this?* If the rightful heirs (sons and daughters) aren't willing to fight with the authority and power we've been given from Dad. If we will fight, we cannot lose.

4 - We ARE NOT Sinners Saved by Grace

The moment we trust and follow Jesus, we are born again. We are not "sinners 2.0," but beloved sons and daughters. *"If anyone is in Christ, he is a new creation. The old is gone; the new has come."* 2 Corinthians 5:17. In fact, skip down to 2 Corinthians 5:21 and we are told that we have become *the righteousness of God. How can I still be a sinner and the righteousness of God at the same time?* It's not biblical.

Do I always act like the righteousness of God? Find me in traffic on I-35 in Dallas and you'll know my behavior doesn't always match this new identity. My identity as a son isn't dependent upon my behavior (Hallelujah!), but the purpose of

God as a disciple is for me to walk more and more like Jesus did…His Son in whom He is well pleased.

Any guesses on which of Paul's New Testament churches is by and large considered the worst? This church entertained sexual immorality of a nature that Paul said would make the pagans blush (1 Corinthians 5:1). *Do you know which one?* It was the church in Corinth. Like a father loving his prodigal group of sons and daughters, Paul went down the line in various areas where they were missing the mark, and not by just a little. Yet, here's how he addresses them:

> To the church of God that is in Corinth, to
> **those sanctified in Christ Jesus, called to**
> **be saints together with all those who in**
> **every place call upon the name of our Lord**
> **Jesus Christ, both their Lord and ours:**
> *1 Corinthians 1:2 (emphasis mine)*

I believe if there's any hope for sons and daughters to walk more and more like Jesus, it'll be because of disciple-makers (spiritual moms and dads…*cause that's how kids are raised, right?*), allowing them to make mistakes…encouraging them in their new identity instead of questioning whether or not they're really saved just because they dirty a diaper or fall back into some of the same mess we found them in.

Many churches only want to modify behavior instead of raising sons and daughters. *I know why.* It's just easier to tell them *what not to do* and hope to catch them again the following Sunday for another lesson. Parents walk with kids and get involved in their messes, even while dealing with their own messes. Mere behavior modification, minus them firmly knowing their true identity, produces pharisees. We must let them get to Dad's heart…even while a long way from home… and begin to concern ourselves with *who they are* instead of *what they merely do*.

Such is good parenting. After all, behavior, while important, is always secondary to identity…our behavior must be formed out of our identity rather than our identity becoming formed out of our behavior. This is discipleship.

5 - Repentance Is for the Church, as Well as the World

I want to re-title the Luke 15 story of the prodigal son to "The Prodigal Sons." The younger leaves his father and squanders his inheritance in wild and lascivious living. He is the clear one to aim the barrel at, *right?* True enough, he lived like hell for a season…indulging in every sensual opportunity, feasting on every lustful opportunity, squandering what Dad had entrusted with him. He's guilty…but that's not *the son* who Jesus was taking aim at in this story.

> Now the tax collectors and sinners were all
> drawing near to hear Him. And the Pharisees
> and the scribes grumbled, saying, "This man
> receives sinners and eats with them." So he
> told them this parable…
> **Luke 15:1–3**

Clearly, Jesus is aiming at the *self-righteous older son* in the story who feels no need to consider his own sinfulness, because he is clearly so much holier than his younger brother. This story ought to give great comfort to folks like us who admit they have fallen short of God's glory, every day, but are willing to turn their hearts toward home.

This story gives no comfort to those who merely compare themselves with others whose lives appear messier than their own. This story was aimed at a religious spirit, which, incidentally, is the most wicked spirit of all. The prostitute may cry, "Lord have mercy on me, a sinner." The tax collectors and the worst of Jesus' day would often cry, "Son of David, have mercy on me." The Pharisee is proud that he is not like the filthy prostitutes and tax collectors.

Throughout the Old Testament, God is continually sending prophets to His people to turn them back from their wickedness…inviting them to repent. At times they'd respond affirmatively, and at other times they'd continue in their open rebellion. Here's the truth, we are either living in repentance or rebellion, but to pretend we don't need the former is rebellion itself. (See 1 John 1:8--10)

> If My people who are called by My name humble
> themselves, and pray and seek My face and
> turn from their wicked ways, then I will hear
> from heaven and will forgive their sins and
> heal their land.
> ***2 Chronicles 7:14***

As evidenced in Luke 15 (above), those who are lost haven't always been so, nor have they lost their worth to the Father. *Just because something is lost doesn't mean it's lost its value.* The son, who'd lived with Dad up until his departure, hadn't lost favor with his father, but had merely lost himself for a time, and his return required him coming to his senses.

Yes, repentance is about our actions, but if our mind hasn't changed, we'll simply go back to what we know/think about ourselves. We need to learn sonship and how to walk in this new identity. Sons run home, even after finding themselves in the filthiest of messes.

In Revelation chapters 2 and 3, Jesus addresses seven churches in Asia Minor. He gives them incredible details about their cities, their works, and their spiritual condition. Seven times, He asks these churches to repent…of sexual immorality…of idolatry…etc. It's clear, we may be already saved and, on His team, but sometimes our behavior isn't acceptable to God as sons and daughters. We must repent.

The idea that a believer can approach an altar once…pray a prayer that Jesus never required of His followers, and then never have to repent again? *Wildly unbiblical.* I'll leave you with just one more reference

> If we say we have no sin, we deceive ourselves,
> and the truth is not in us. If we confess our
> sins, he is faithful and just to forgive us our
> sins and to cleanse us from all
> unrighteousness. If we say we have not

sinned, we make him a liar, and his word is
not in us.
1 John 1:8–10

6 - Judge vs Father

Is God a judge? Absolutely…

Then I saw a great white throne and him who
was seated on it. From his presence earth and
sky fled away, and no place was found for
them. And I saw the dead, great and small,
standing before the throne, and books were
opened. Then another book was opened,
which is the book of life. And the dead were
judged by what was written in the
books, according to what they had done.
Revelation 20:11–12

However, this is not the relationship He has chosen to have
with us. In Christ Jesus, He becomes our Father… we are adopted
and have a new name… and a new relationship with Dad.

Jesus never taught His disciples to pray to, *"Our Judge who
art in heaven,"* but to *our Father*. We will run from a judge
because we know good and well that our actions, even as sons
and daughters, make us guilty at times. A judge isn't safe when
you're guilty. So, as sons and daughters who find the pigpen
from time to time, we know it's safe to run to a Father who

loves us so much that He even sent His own Son to redeem us from the conditions He finds us in.

So, who faces the Judge? It is not sons, but those who have rejected Jesus Christ as their Lord.

> He who has the Son has life. He who does not
> have the Son does not have life; the wrath of
> God remains upon him.
> **John 3:36**

As believers, our works will be judged (see 2 Corinthians 5:10), but as sons and daughters, Jesus already paid the bill off entirely for our admittance into His kingdom. There is *nothing held against us.*

> ...no longer counting men's trespasses against
> them.
> **2 Corinthians 5:17**

And...

> ...God made Him who knew no sin, to become
> sin for us, that in Him, we might become the
> righteousness of God.
> **2 Corinthians 5:21**

When our trespasses are no longer counted by God, we no longer need to fear a judge, but can run to the arms of our Father. As the righteousness of God (which is one of the hardest biblical truths for us to embrace, especially when our behavior isn't holy) we have no fear of judgment. Indeed, for all in Christ Jesus, there is no judgment day…that bill got paid nearly 2000 years ago. It was a prisoner exchange of the highest order.

> …whoever hears My word and believes Him
> who sent Me has eternal life. He does not
> come into judgment, but has passed from
> death to life.
> ### John 5:24

7 - Salvation Cost Jesus His Life; Discipleship Costs Us Ours

> Have this mind among yourselves, which is
> yours in Christ Jesus, who, though He was
> in the form of God, did not count equality
> with God a thing to be grasped, but emptied
> Himself, by taking the form of a servant,
> being born in the likeness of men. And being
> found in human form, He humbled himself
> by becoming obedient to the point of
> death, even death on a cross. Therefore God
> has highly exalted Him and bestowed on
> Him the name that is above every name, so
> that at the name of Jesus every knee should
> bow, in heaven and on earth and under the
> earth, and every tongue confess that Jesus
> Christ is Lord, to the glory of God the Father.
> ### Philippians 2:5–11

So what did Jesus give up to become fully man? The answer I hear most often to this question is "His deity." This isn't true. You can't be deity and then become non-deity...your nature is or isn't deity. There are too many Scriptures pointing to the deity of Jesus, as well as His humanity. *So what did He leave behind?* The answer to that question lies in understanding exactly what He asks each of His followers/disciples to give up.

> If anyone would come after me, let him deny
> himself and take up his cross daily and follow
> me. For whoever would save his life will lose
> it, but whoever loses his life for my sake will
> save it. For what does it profit a man if he
> gains the whole world and loses or forfeits
> himself?
> **Luke 9:23–27**

Jesus left the life He had in heaven behind Him and gave up His *rights*...His desire to please *self*...to put *self-first*. He was entitled to the throne He sat on prior to coming to be born of a virgin. He was entitled to all the benefits of Lordship yet made Himself a servant. In fact, unlike a lot of business cards with fancy titles in the church world today, Jesus rarely, if ever, flashed the "Son of God" card, but instead used the title "Son of Man" prolifically.

When Satan tempted Jesus in the wilderness for forty days and nights, he was provoking Jesus to appeal to His own will instead of the Father's will. In discipleship, He asks us to deny

our*selves* and commit to doing His will as He denied Himself
and did the Father's will.

> For I have come down from heaven, not to do
> My own will but the will of Him who
> sent Me.
> **John 6:38**

Jesus so emptied Himself of any of His rights and privileges
as God, that He became completely dependent upon the Father
to do any of the miracles He did. This is an example for us that
He wasn't doing miracles just because He could, but because He
prayed and the Father heard His prayers…meaning, the reason
we often don't see miracles has nothing to do with the fact that
we aren't deity, but because we don't depend on the Father
enough in prayer and His word. Our power comes from prayer
(Matthew 17:21); our authority comes from the Word (John
12:49).

Once again, by way of reminder, salvation came at the cost
of Jesus' life; discipleship comes at the cost of our lives. Let me
give you a couple quick examples from Scripture.

In Genesis 12, Abram was given a promise from God that he
would be the father of many nations. With this promise in hand,
he left everything in his homeland and took God at His word…
everything promised was contingent upon a son. He would wait
decades…even having his name changed to "Abraham"
meaning *"father of many nations"*…all the while without a son.

He would carry his own name like a badge that belonged to
someone else, because he had no child…no realized blessing…

no nations calling him "father."   When God finally visited
Abraham and Sarah and made good on His promise of giving
Abraham a son, He was already one hundred years old. And
then, after waiting to become a father, God asks Abraham to
sacrifice the boy on an altar in Genesis 22.

Abraham had waited decades and now, upon receiving the
promise of a son, Isaac…God now requires Isaac as an offering
back to Him. Every promise God had given Abraham was
centered on this kid…the dream of being a father…the promise
of nations coming from him… blessings upon blessings for the
world… and now God says, after giving him a son, *"Take him
and sacrifice him"*…i.e. *"lose your life."*

Abraham's life and hopes were bound up in the boy he
would bind and place upon the altar. I'm convinced the easier
ask of Abraham would've been to ask him to sacrifice himself
instead of his son of blessing and promise. God was asking
Abraham to lay his *life and dreams* down in obedience. As the
father of the faith, Abraham never hesitated but trusted God and
obeyed.

*So too, Jesus' disciples never walked away from empty nets
to follow Him.*

In Luke chapter 5, Jesus calls a fisherman named Peter to
follow Him. Peter fished; he just wasn't any good at it. I'm
certain Peter had dreamed of the day he would catch so many
fish that he was the envy of every other fisherman on the Sea of
Galilee. *What fisherman doesn't?* His life and dreams were
bound up in what could be caught and hauled within the
dimensions of his nets and boat.

Had Jesus wanted to make it easy on Peter, He'd have asked

him to leave his empty nets on the shore of the sea and fall in line behind Him. Instead, He calls the fisherman out into the deep waters and proceeds to exceed any fishing dream Peter had ever dreamed before. Jesus fills his boats with so many fish that two boats begin to sink under the weight of this catch. It wasn't until Peter had everything he'd ever dreamed of…right there in his boat… that Jesus asked him to lay his life and dreams aside, and to dream a new dream.

Peter *lost his life* that day, embarked on a new life, and began to dream a new dream. While others were on the beach counting the fish he'd just caught, Peter was nowhere to be found. He'd laid aside his old life to follow Jesus.

8 - Jesus Leaves the Ninety-Nine to Find the One… He Also Asks the One to Leave the Ninety-Nine

Pay attention to the crowd factor throughout the Gospels. At times the crowds around Jesus are in the way of folks getting to Him for healing. At other times the crowd is fair weather or fickle, committed to a good meal or a display of the miraculous, but not committed to following Jesus. Yes, they'd listen to the message, place a little money in the basket, but Jesus knew that outside of discipleship (laying down one's life to follow Jesus), most would merely supplement their week with a good message or two, yet retain their own way of living.

One of the greatest gifts God gives to His children is the opportunity to stand for Him when no one else around is willing to do so. *Why?* Because in those moments, we find out a lot about whose approval we are truly seeking. I vividly remember a few of these formative moments in undergraduate and graduate school, where what felt like persecution from the crowd was the fire in which God used to fashion something in me that didn't require their approval... *just His*.

Jesus called Peter away from the crowd of fish-counters to follow Him... to become a fisher of men. He called Paul to leave the fraternal ranks of the religious elites in Jerusalem to follow Him across Asia Minor... spending his life as an outcast and even a prisoner. Praise God for those moments He grants us the privilege of standing alone before a scoffing crowd to please Him alone.

I remember an event that occurred shortly after I decided at age nineteen to follow Jesus. Standing between our home and the church my father pastored, I was greeted by four friends who were encouraging me to attend a nearby strip club with them. Although I had never done so previously, it was something that would've intrigued me just months earlier... before I decided to follow Jesus. My new commitment had so strained my relationship with one of these guys that he threatened the following:

"We know you're doing this new religious thing, but we're your friends. Mike, you're going to have to choose. It's us or Jesus."

I chose Jesus, and while I have failed Him so many times along the way, that decision proved consequential because it was the first of many times, I was confronted with the decision to lay my old life aside, to put Him first. One of my four guys standing there that night is a dear friend named Keith. He would call me a year and a half later, telling me that I must've really found something great if I was willing to lose my best friends over it. *I had.* Keith said it was that "losing everything for Jesus" moment in the yard that caused him to search his own heart. He told me he'd given his life to Jesus to find the same treasure I'd found.

9 - Power Comes from Prayer; Authority Comes from the Word of God

Everything Jesus did was in relationship with His Father. This was the pattern. I'm not against a stage, but it can never replace an altar. I'm not against a smoke machine or the best lighting a church can afford, but nothing replaces the presence of the Holy Spirit.

I'm 100 percent for contending for the faith publicly, but it will never be effective without first contending for it privately… in that quiet space Jesus often found alone with Dad. Satan would much rather have us keep it all public, but that's what Jesus warned any old Pharisee was willing to do…everything for show.

Prayer is our source of power. Once, when Jesus' disciples were unsuccessfully attempting to cast out a demon, they inquired as to why Jesus could do this, and they could not. Keep in mind, His response wasn't, *"Because I'm the Son of God and you aren't,"* but rather:

And he said to them, "This kind cannot be driven out by anything but prayer."

Mark 9:29

We can do everything Jesus told us we can do, but His answer was simple: PRAYER.

As a young seminarian, I once read a Leonard Ravenhill quote that stuck with me:

"No man is greater than his prayer life."

This is true of any church or ministry. We might get folks inspired, but the Holy Spirit is the One who transforms in our own quiet time. If we abdicate this area in our life, we find ourselves trying to do the heavy lifting that God has promised was His responsibility alone. He is the One who instructs us privately about anything we feel we are called to do publicly.

In fact, there are three areas of personal discipleship that are non-negotiables for anyone who calls himself or herself a disciple: a commitment to the WORD… a commitment to WORSHIP… a commitment to PRAYER. No disciple can lay aside any of these three areas and remain true to the call of discipleship.

10 - Forgiveness vs Healing

Forgiveness of our sins is a *vertical relationship* we have with the Father through Jesus Christ. He paid the bill off entirely at the tree…we don't need to go to a pastor, evangelist, or priest, but to the Father Himself in prayer:

If we confess our sins, He is faithful and just to

forgive us our sins, and cleanse us from all
unrighteousness.
1 John 1:9

God is in the forgiving business. In fact, He is far more
committed to our forgiveness than we are. He wants us saved far
more than we want to be saved. He isn't stingy with this act but *paid
for it in blood...the blood of His own Son. "He is willing that none
should perish, but that all should come to repentance"* (2 Peter 3:9).

Healing is a *horizontal relationship* we have with other
disciples. This isn't to say that there aren't times where God
doesn't unilaterally bring us healing, but *His instruction* is as
follows:

> Confess your sins one to another, so that you may
> be healed.
> ***James 5:16***

The greatest revivals the church has witnessed have two
things in common: *steadfast prayer* and *open repentance of sin*
before God and others. The moment we open our mouths about
our sin, we begin to find the healing that God has for us. This
isn't a quick process... or a *one and done*, but one that must
become a pattern in our lives.

> For when I kept silent, my bones wasted away
> through my groaning all day long. For day
> and night your hand was heavy upon me; my

strength was dried up as by the heat of
summer. I acknowledged my sin to you, and I
did not cover my iniquity; I said, "I will
confess my transgressions to the Lord," and
you forgave the iniquity of my sin.
Psalm 32:3–5

And...

Whoever conceals his transgressions will not
prosper, but he who confesses and forsakes
them will obtain mercy.
Proverbs 28:13

If, as disciples, we feel we cannot admit to the truth about
our mess, the following verses apply:

If we say we have no sin, we deceive ourselves,
and the truth is not in us... If we say we have
not sinned, we make him a liar, and his word
is not in us.
1 John 1:8, 10

If is the biggest and most consequential word in the Bible.
The *if* is all about obedience.

In the past three years, I've ministered in bars and VFWs
where I can testify, you may not find *truth* in those places, but
you'll often find folks who are far more *honest* about their mess.

Sometimes, church is the last place people can be honest about their struggles.

My encouragement to anyone reading this is to find someone out ahead of you in the faith…someone who won't publicly announce your failure or push you further under the water when you're already drowning in whatever area, but who will dry you off and help you to start again. Let them encourage you, even with the word "NO" at times.

Find a black belt in the faith and ask to be discipled. Admit where you're still failing, and ultimately healing… over time and through prayer… will be the result. Like playing football on a sprained ankle, we are going to need to lean on the good ankle for some time… and that's why God gives us someone stronger than ourselves to lean upon. It's God's model and He will always kiss His own Word.

10

BROTHER BROTHER

The wrestler stepped right up to Kevin, within intimate proximity, whereupon Kevin leaned forward, kissed him on the mouth, and threw one of the greatest uppercuts I've personally witnessed.

Before Ellis and Helen Ryherd, there was just Kevin. *That thought didn't dawn on me until this morning in the shower.* This thought, unearthed because of the nature of this writing, was immediately unsettling for me because it meant we were on our own at ages no infant or toddler should be alone.

I don't remember life before Mom and Dad, but Kevin (nearly twelve months older than me) does. After all, I was seven months and eight days old when we got saved (by Mom and Dad)... Kevin had absorbed nearly two years.

I don't remember Kevin (or anything else) during this time, but he said he remembers me, not vividly perhaps, because it's hard to cognitively capture much by age two, but it tells me he must've felt very alone, because he was aware enough to know we simply had each other... and prior to my arrival, it was just him.

Aside from severely traumatic events, the average individual doesn't begin processing much prior to the age of three, but the events we endured were severely traumatic. (This is true for our siblings who stayed longer in Jimmy and Vickie's *care*.)

I've had a couple experts express to me that we both likely suffer from some level of attachment issues because of this affection deficiency in our formative stages, but my faith tells me that whatever transpired prior to our exodus from the Jimmy and Vickie system, no longer applies to our lives after our adoption. Any stronghold over us was broken the day we were delivered from our bondage.

Any scars of this era are merely reminders of our redemption, not shackles dooming our present and future. Our past was purchased for $600, and that's where it ended.

Kevin and I will always be brothers, with a bond that will never be broken. Growing up, we had moments where this bond was tested and weakened, but never broken. Months, especially after an explosive episode of left hooks, straight jabs, and a few broken noses, we wouldn't speak.

All this ultimately gave way to the reality that we are brothers who endured far worse from those who really didn't care if we lived or died. We've always cared for each other.

Kevin was a hero to me growing up, as big brothers often are to little brothers. To this day, neither of us has felt a need to become the softest petal on the flower, simply because we love Jesus…and we both do. We both excelled at sports and things masculine in nature.

We both held our own in situations requiring physical confrontation, and *provided the cause was just*, wouldn't back down because of our resolve to fight well when the situation required it of us.

We have a code: we don't fear losing a fight, *we fear not fighting* when we are called to do so. I believe more men need to fear cowardice and having a fear of man rather than a right fear of God…even a willingness for the occasional fist fight (yes, *provided the cause is just* for some of you who need to hear that again).

David was such a man. Saul's army feared a man (Goliath) while David feared God and nothing else. As Paul the apostle contended in 1 Corinthians 16:13–14, "…act like men."

For us, having grown up in the home of our father who'd been born in poverty in 1928, we didn't go to the hospital for much of anything. Again, with Dad, nothing short of a severed

limb required a trip to the emergency room. *Think I'm kidding?*
One day in 1978 Kevin and I got into an argument, and I started
to climb a tree to get away from him because he was bigger and
stronger at this time.

As I struggled to get to the next branch, I felt his grip on
my right ankle, and the sudden awareness I couldn't pull the
both of us upward. I hit the ground with a thud. Nearly
unconscious, I remember Kevin running from me to the front
door of our home in Newton, Iowa, only to faintly see my
mother emerge, disappear, and then reemerge with a soaked
washcloth. My left eyeball had dislodged from its socket
because of the impact from my landing and was just hanging
there by the optic nerve.

Kevin was in a panic, but Mom simply approached me,
placed the wetted cloth over my eye, and started to pray. I don't
remember any pain, just the intensity of her prayer standing in
our front yard that afternoon. When she finally removed her
hand from my face, I knew her prayer must've been answered,
because she began to praise God for my healing.

Kevin, however, didn't start to praise God, but felt he was
likely going to experience something just shy of the wrath of
God from Mom. She beat his butt. *I still don't believe she did it
nearly hard enough.* Ultimately, there was no hospital bill
because we never went.

One snow-covered morning on the playground of Cody
Elementary School in North Platte, Nebraska, Kevin broke his
collarbone while playing football. Knowing, even at this age,
neither of us would leave the field of play for anything shy of
those *severed limbs* I've just mentioned, I accompanied my

brother to the nurse's office, knowing he had to be seriously injured.

The same kid who'd just got the drop on Kevin moments earlier, causing him to hit the ground, cracking his shoulder, was now walking beside us, taunting Kevin as he made his way inside our school building.

A few feet from the entrance where I was holding the door, Kevin's attention momentarily shifted back to this kid still mouthing threats toward him, and my brother threw a straight jab at his jaw, with his good arm, knocking him down on the icy sidewalk. That was the stuff of legend to a younger brother.

By the time we'd both graduated high school, I'd watched him get punched in the mouth by a middle schooler whose punch drew significant blood, upon which Kevin immediately spit a mouthful of blood into the kid's eyes and commenced to pummel him.

A few years later, I watched him step into a fight in a parking lot in Oskaloosa, Iowa, because a wrestler was threatening me. The wrestler stepped right up to Kevin, within intimate proximity, whereupon Kevin leaned forward, kissed him on the mouth, and threw one of the greatest uppercuts I've personally witnessed. That ended it.

To this day, I appreciate good men willing to do some things considered pretty bad... *provided the cause is just*. There is no virtue in weakness, but in meekness. There is no sin in strength, just when used wickedly, especially to hurt women, children and those who are weaker just to demonstrate one's strength.

As sociologist Jordan Peterson suggests, *"A harmless man is a dangerous man."* This doesn't conflict with my Christian theology whatsoever, though it often gets me a few sideways looks from other believers who don't see it that way.

Yes, Mom struggled with our excessive testosterone. She was outnumbered by us boys, and, from about age fourteen or so, was too undersized to physically rectify an intense situation between Kevin and me. In our home, there was no Atari or Xbox, it was baseballs and footballs, BB guns and dirt clod wars.

We lived outside as boys where we broke arms and fingers, and occasionally a window playing baseball, but in her world, it was preferable to her chandelier or our bedroom sheetrock...but that's not what got to Mom the most.

It was our words...often cuss words. Her reflexes were insanely feline when it came to us mouthing off, and whatever speed a cat bats at a nearby shiny object, Mom seemed faster. As a woman now undersized by two boys who played college football, when it came to cussing or mouthing off, there was no easing up on the gas, it was usually a straight backhand at the speed of light...even breaking her fingers a time or two. *Money shots.*

We knew we deserved every one of them...and a whole lot more for the things she never heard. As she aged, when Kevin and I felt she was getting a little too bossy or sassy, we would nod at one another and simply sandwich her in a hug that way the white filling is sandwiched between the chocolatey outer layers of an Oreo cookie. *Did she protest? Absolutely.* We'd just wait it out...until her arms stopped flailing and she'd finally stopped hollering. These *sandwich hugs* are some of our favorite memories with Mom.

Mom died from cancer at the age of seventy-one in 2002 in her home in Elgin, North Dakota. I'd just turned twenty-nine and Kevin had just turned thirty. I keenly remember as a child thinking my parents, who were often mistaken as our grandparents whenever we went out to eat or shop or whatever, might die before my friends' parents…because they were older when they got us. When she died, I remember it felt like suffocation to me.

My parents, unlike many of my friends' accounts, were my best friends. There was no childhood friend who could compete with the level of love and grace my parents continually offered us…and as boys, we never openly shared the details of what Dad had described upon finding us, *but internally, we never forgot.* There was seemingly no happy ending to our story minus these two heroes.

As I'd mentioned, Mom was near perfect as a girl for her parents. After nearly three decades with her before she went to heaven, I still don't have ANY dirt on her to share with y'all to make this part of the story more compelling. But in the absence of any real crime or even minor offenses, let me offer this as a disingenuous criticism of my mom.

I shared at her funeral in March of 2002 that she'd made my high school football tapes unwatchable. In Eddyville, Iowa, I was an option quarterback, who, because of my position on the field, touched the ball on every single offensive play, and whose mom knew virtually nothing about football, except that I had the ball every play.

Her proximity to Dad, who was recording my games with a VHS camera, produced a cacophonous and shrill mix of excited and rabid, "*Go Michael, Go Michael, Go Michael…oh no… Go Michael*" on not one, but every play…*every play*.

When my buddies and I would attempt to watch the game footage my dad had captured the previous weekend, almost instinctively, we'd turn the sound off. Mom didn't understand football, but based on that level of support alone, *on every play*, I understood she loved me (and Kevin) with every breath she took. I believe, according to Hebrews 12:1, she is in heaven's stands, annoying each person beside her as I write this, because she hasn't stopped rooting for Kevin, me, and our families. *Mom, please don't stop rooting for us down here… not until the whistle blows.*

I never saw my dad walk on water, but he walked in such a way that I knew God was real. Kevin was Momma's boy, and I was Dad's kid. We all understood this within our home, particularly as we grew into young adults. Kevin would drive Mom and Dad far crazier than I ever did, but I believe she feigned outrage while privately rejoicing he was becoming his own man. Dad shared no such joy, which is probably why he found me the more reasonable choice.

Dad threw the ball for Kevin and me, even into his sixties, because he'd raised us to love Jesus and play football. Countless nights of playing catch together in our yard across decades, our nightly anthem when his aging arm would start to tire: "Just one more, Dad."

I'm certain us boys were out throwing him by the time we hit middle school, but he made time for us… and we never let him leave throwing the ball with us (and retreat to his nightly chair) without protesting his evening retirement.

I was standing with my dad one spring afternoon in our gravel driveway in Belle Fourche, South Dakota. It was the first time I ever remember being pissed off at God. Standing next to him, I remember I was cool with Dad, but this day, God and I had beef. You see, Dad had extended his arms to me as a three-year-old at the end of the diving board at our YMCA in Newton, Iowa.

I jumped, and like Dad promised, I didn't die, but he caught me. He'd extended his arms to me as an eight-year-old to join him in the baptismal pool the day he baptized me. He told Kevin and me we could trust Jesus in good and bad times, just like the Shepherd in Psalm 23 could be trusted. Now, I was thirteen years old and needed track cleats. Dad was in his late fifties and was serving a church that had just cut his pay and our medical insurance.

Why wasn't Anyone there to catch Dad? Where were the green pastures and still waters that a life of following God guarantees? Don't let me fool you: as a thirteen-year-old, *the bigger issue for me was the cleats.* One line from Dad will stay with me forever:

"Michael, I don't have the money right now, but if you really need them, I'll find it."

How? How could a red pair of $20 New Balance cleats disturb our financial serenity? How could serving God into his fifties have such a small return on investment? I was aggravated that I couldn't buy something so mundane, but my heart was cut deeply by his honesty and commitment to helping me *at such great cost* to him.

. . .

At thirteen, I never considered how much this admission might have broken him, I was mostly concerned with my own momentary disappointment. My selfishness allowed me to only see myself, but his pained words lodged in my ears until years later when they found some fertile ground within my heart.

"I will never go into ministry," I told my thirteen-year-old self that day.

11

THE CHAPTER I DIDN'T WANT TO WRITE

...this conversation would bring an ending to more than just a marriage that had been on life support, it would take with it every dream we'd shared, at one point or another, about what we'd hoped it might be together.

"You're mad at me."

"No, I'm pissed."

For the time-being, our dialogue would have to end there. After all, the last song of our morning worship was almost finished and, like most Sundays for the last twenty-plus years, I was preaching that morning. I collected myself from the floor near the stage and dried a few tears that I'd best describe as a swill of hurt and anger and disappointment and bitterness.

"I should have never gone into ministry," I told my forty-six-year-old self.

Dad passed away on February 3, 2019. Before his death, he'd spent the month of January with me in Texas. I'm forever grateful for the trips he and I would take when he came to Texas, especially this one. We journeyed to the Valley of Texas, where he grew up and he and Mom pastored their second church in the 1950s. I remember him telling me how, as a young pastor, he and Mom had struggled so in those early years.

Once while pastoring a church in Edinburg, he and Mom ventured up to Victoria, Texas, where they spent a week at a revival with a woman evangelist. At some point the evangelist and Dad were corresponding when she said something that provoked my Dad to utter, *"Never have truer words been spoken through falser teeth." Normally, that'd be funny.*

However, she immediately burst into tears and left my mom and dad standing alone, wondering what had caused her emotional outburst and quick departure. It turned out, she had false teeth and was extremely self-conscious about anyone finding this out. *Who am I kidding? It's funny.*

Arriving in Edinburg on our last trip together, we drove to the site of the church, and he was surprised to see it was still standing. The building looked unkempt and as if it should've been razed decades earlier. Dad cried. I didn't cry, but I was moved by his tears.

I couldn't help but think that while our growing up years were slim financially, Mom and Dad had seen tougher times. And yet, they welcomed us boys.

In the words uttered by one of my best friends at his own mother's funeral, where he spoke as an eighteen–year–old who'd just lost any parental stability his own single parent household had afforded him growing up, *"Mom was Walmart so we could be Nike."* Those words resonated with me deeply and are forever etched into my own story now.

Whether self-imposed, or a byproduct of a religious system (or some combination of both) pastors are conditioned to hide any personal struggles, especially their own shortcomings, i.e. sin. Oh yes, it's there, and it's unfair to them, because the only way we overcome these areas is by opening our mouths in confession (James 5:16).

Privately, as a pastor, I had struggled at varying levels with pornography, but at the core of this struggle, there was a marriage in free fall. Yes, my ex-wife had brought her own baggage to our relationship, but I'd opened a door to sexual immorality prior to meeting her.

When intimacy was cut off in our marriage, *for all the reasons we always seemed to find,* porn became my retreat. *"If she is unwilling to meet this need, I know another way,"* I told myself. Masturbation was my comfort food. When I got hungry enough, I ate… and always felt like throwing up afterward. I was a hypocrite.

By 2017, we seriously discussed the divorce that was regularly threatened in what became more and more frequent arguments. In one of our last family meetings, I remember coming home one evening and having everyone seated in our living room. I wasn't willing to live any longer under the threat of divorce.

It was the first time in our home that my children heard me

cuss. I wasn't innocent, but I knew we both had to make seismic changes for our family to have any chance at restoration. The foundations were faulty, and my job as the head of our family was to rip them up in the hopes of setting a new groundwork.

"If you're going to leave, leave. If you're going to stay, stay...but don't ever threaten me with divorce again. That shit is toxic. We both need to repent and renounce the sin we've brought into this union."

My hope was that this statement would prove consequential enough that, for better or worse, decisions would be made. It proved consequential, but not as I hoped. The divide only widened, and bitterness ensued. What I'd privately prayed for years for God to heal, now became conspicuous enough that those surrounding us couldn't help but see our situation was critical.

I can honestly say there were moments when we both tried to make it work, but the damage was irreconcilable. I failed.

I'd prided myself as a quarterback who could lead ten other guys down a field in unity. I'd taken pride in the fact that as a young pastor, I could lead a congregation well. I was very proud that, despite my coaching deficiencies, I'd started a program for kids who needed hugs and a father figure more than touchdowns. As it pertained to my wife, I had failed, and I was ashamed and bitter.

In late 2018, the lure of images on a screen was no longer enough. I wanted to be touched again. I desired to feel a woman's touch. Touch, including sexual intimacy, was a thing of the past in our marriage. I wanted to be wanted *that way* again. And yes, I didn't want to consider a life without sex, which we'd been living.

Instead of going to God, I went to a massage parlor knowing full well that if I walked through the door, part of what I'd hoped for would be granted. I entered the dimly lit parlor, hoping for a feminine touch and a hand job. I requested and received both.

> So when the woman saw that the tree was good
>   for food, and that it was a delight to the
>   eyes...she took of its fruit and ate.
> **Genesis 3:6**

Something that can look so good, when we seek it outside of God's provision, brings death. *(I understand that must sound preachy and hypocritical at this juncture, but it's still true.)*

Death resulted...just not immediately. Initially, I didn't run home and confess my sin. I stayed up night after night wrestling with thoughts of shame and betrayal...because I had tasted forbidden fruit, and I had no rest. *I was guilty as sin.*

The man others had looked to for spiritual guidance and leadership was the man I couldn't look at in the mirror. The dad that seemed to be a constant among the many variables in my kids' lives was no longer credible. The husband who had vowed faithfulness to my wife was unfaithful.

The temporary satisfaction I'd experienced was fleeting, while the guilt was lasting. To console myself, across the next several weeks, I'd return to the scene of the crime as a repeat offender. All the while, I was certain that any revelation of these acts would immediately be the final straw for our marriage. *I was right.*

It would be the last time I sat with my wife together in our living room in Corinth, Texas. Yes, we've had cordial moments since, but this conversation would bring an ending to more than just a marriage that had been on life support, it would take with it every dream we'd shared, at one point or another, about what we'd hoped it might be *together.*

"The reason I haven't been sleeping at night is because I did something that I know is going to hurt you… pause …I went to a massage parlor and had a woman give me a happy ending."

There was no yelling. When she asked if I'd done this more than once, I immediately lied and told her it had only happened once, so as not to compound an already volatile situation. Internally, my hope was that if I could find some measure of grace for my transgression, I would ultimately admit to all of it. Without any discernible emotion, she responded:

"I'm leaving you."

……(2:30 a.m. that next morning)……

"Dad, get up!" my youngest demanded.

After our conversation, even in the light of an imminent divorce, a weight had at least partly lifted off me so that I slept like I hadn't in weeks. Now, abruptly awakened, I walked downstairs where I saw my wife seated beside all three of our girls. Just hours before I'd dropped a bomb that would forever damage any hopes of our reconciliation.

Questions didn't come from my ex, but from my girls, and they were rightfully devastated and enraged:

"How could you find a girl, one probably our age, as a man of God, and have sex with her?"

"People look to you as a pastor."

"How could you betray Mom and each of us?"

I didn't attempt to respond to every question, but felt they needed me to acknowledge to them that I had done this, and I did. At this moment, I felt my words would prove impotent in assuaging the betrayal and hurt they each felt, so I kept my words limited, knowing their anger was completely justified. They were right and I was wrong.

In all my forty-six years (at that time), there was never a time where I felt more like a ship lost at sea than that moment. I'd give up any church, any friendship, any accolade…for them. It's not even a contest, and in that moment, it wasn't just my wife who I felt was exiting the family frame, I felt them slipping away too.

Lying prostrate on the gray carpet of the church that Sunday morning in February of 2019, as I wiped away tears and attempted to collect myself, I reminded God that I was sorry for the damage I'd done…that I'd justified my sin because of my own hurt…that I'd selfishly sought out my own satisfaction at the expense of my family…and I knew nothing would ever be the same.

While God, according to His promise in 1 John 1:9, removed my sin and shame, another emotion remained. Anger. Not God's. *Mine.*

"I know I sinned against You, against my wife… against my family… but I also know I prayed for years for my spouse and my marriage…for our home…for these girls… day after day

after day. Yes, I was unfaithful, but I thought you'd faithfully heal what I'd been crying out to You for all those years. I did pray… I fasted… I trusted You to do Your part. Why does it feel like You never answered those prayers?"

"You're mad at me." (This was perhaps the closest I've heard to the audible voice of God.)

"No, I'm pissed."

12

DESERT ROSE

At once, yet again, I was angry. That's not how you're supposed to handle this, I thought. I need your chastisement, your stern disapproval, your severe displeasure... Let's get on with it... Tell me I'm disqualified and make it quick because I'm already broken. I'd rather not linger here.

Within a week after my initial confession to my wife and my girls, my dad arrived at our home in Texas. Before his arrival, he was unaware of my transgression and the new reality of an upcoming divorce. He was ninety, and as hard as it was going to be *on me* to share this news with him, I was concerned about its effect on him. Physically, he was already failing, and I was about to break his heart.

Dad and I loved to spend our mornings at Rudy's BBQ in Denton, where we'd each grab a couple brisket, egg, and cheese tacos, as well as several cups of their pecan praline coffee. *If they don't serve Rudy's breakfast tacos in heaven…? I don't even want to think about that.*

When we'd arrived back at the house, I paused before helping him get his seat belt unfastened.

I laid everything out in front of him, with all the sordid details, and then punctuated our conversation with this:

"Dad, we are getting a divorce."

Without any hesitation, he turned his head, smiled at me, and simply said:

"Michael, I love you."

I'll carry those words with me forever. It was as true in that moment as the first time he'd ever spoken such words to me, and it came when I needed it the most. Kevin and I needed that love from Mom and Dad as infants, but I'm convinced I needed it every bit as badly in the driveway that day.

Just outside my driver's door in our driveway, my ex-wife had planted rose bushes. I was no fan. *Why?* Because one of those bushes, proximate to where my car door would open, was a little overgrown and would snag my clothes if I wasn't paying attention to my steps or particularly skinny enough to step around it that day. As I said, I wasn't in the habit of cussing, but that rose bush often had me thinking about a variety of different cuss words I'd like to have used if I was in the habit of using them.

While I loved having Dad with me, I felt the timing was awful. I'd just been served notice within a week of his arrival that life as we'd known it was coming to an end. I needed space to process and navigate what my next steps were, *and Dad needed his belt unbuckled.* I needed to discuss my resignation with church elders, *and Dad needed help up the stairs of our home.*

I was in the middle of a tsunami *and Dad needed someone to put his shoes on, button his shirts and comb his hair.* For the most part, I was joyful in this service, but there were moments where I felt overwhelmed by everything that seemed to be falling apart around me, in addition to whatever he needed at any given moment…even a few regrettable moments of outright impatience on my part. I felt snagged by little requests when I wanted a little space to consider my own dilemma.

Roses don't bloom in January. That kind of thing occurs in late March or well into April in Texas. While Dad was staying with us that month, the rose bush that had aggravated me so mercilessly (not unlike the way I occasionally became aggravated at the simplest of his requests) decided to bloom on a single stem, producing one red rose.

It'd never happened before, and I promise you I would've noticed because I was always watching my steps along that well-worn path to our door. In hindsight, I consider it was God's sign to me that amongst what is considered dead/dormant, He is resurrecting life. Amongst the pain and cuts, He is offering healing. His way may not be around the thorns, but through them.

A few weeks later, I stood before his casket telling of how he and Mom had rescued Kevin and me so long ago, and, taped to the inside cover of my Bible, was, and remains, this rose.

Dad had finally hung up his jersey. While I was rejoicing, he wasn't suffering any more, internally I was reeling because I was as wounded in the game of life as I'd ever been, and the man who was the constant in all the variables of my life was gone. God's timing for all these events seemed bad.

Within the same week in January that Dad had come to visit, I sat down with the leadership of our church in Flower Mound, Texas and detailed the events of my fall. I remember two of our elders, upon hearing the details initially, met with me at a nearby pancake house. Whether they came to this decision mutually or individually, I'm not certain, but they decided to help in the restoration of my life and ministry, and I'm forever grateful for their decision. I was brought close instead of pushed away.

Roughly a month later I would find myself at another pancake house in Grapevine, Texas. My mentor and spiritual father, Larry Titus, met me at the host's desk. Normally, we'd get to the table and have ordered our drinks before he says something completely mind blowing. Not this day. When asked "How many?" by the hostess, he replied in words I could barely stomach:

"Table for me and my son," he replied.

Son? Why did he have to say that? I'm about to share with

him every reason why I don't deserve to be called "son," and he goes there? (internally) *Let's get this over quickly and I'll probably never see him again.*

"So tell me what's happened," he inquired.

"*I went to some massage parlors...got a few 'happy endings' ...I came home and told the family...and now the divorce is all but final,*" I answered as quickly as possible, bracing for whatever I knew I had coming to me. What he said next hit me harder than anything I'd imagined he might say to me.

"*I'm so proud of you,*" he shot back.

At once, yet again, I was angry. *That's not how you're supposed to handle this,* I thought. *I need your chastisement, your stern disapproval, your severe displeasure... Let's get on with it... Tell me I'm disqualified and make it quick because I'm already broken. I'd rather not linger here.*

"*Did you even listen to what I just said!*" I protested.

"*I'm so proud of you. You didn't have to confess to your wife and kids. You didn't have to confess to me. You could have been at any other Cracker Barrel this morning. You didn't have to show up here this morning. What's done is done, and now, you're not running from it, but facing it.*"

Seated in a chair that I was ready to abandon prior to the arrival of any coffee or pancakes (immediately following my confession), I felt like the younger son in Luke 15. The son who'd assumed, and even postured himself, for his father's rejection. Yet, instead of being turned away, he was embraced, receiving a kiss and a robe from his father.

Moments earlier, I was keenly aware of the stain and stench

of the pigpen I had soiled myself in, but my spiritual dad embraced me at my weakest moment and made me aware of something greater than my sin. He made me aware of his love… and it eclipsed my mess.

As disciples of Jesus, our behavior is important…but thankfully (because our behavior doesn't always match our beliefs), it doesn't singularly define our relationship with God. Our *identity* in Him as sons and daughters is the foundational requisite for God's acceptance of us. This truth doesn't condone or justify our sinful behavior, but instead, it transforms us to live out of an identity that enables us to walk as Jesus walked. Identity must never flow out of behavior; behavior must flow out of identity.

While the leadership at the church I led hadn't turned me away either, *the embrace of a father was critical for me.* In fact, the heart of discipleship is positioning ourselves under another who is out ahead of us. One who spiritually parents us toward maturity. I understand how rare this is, but true discipleship will never occur simply from a pulpit down to a pew.

This is why every born-again believer needs a discipler in his or her life immediately… not just sermons. We can grow in knowledge, but a spiritual father or mother walks beside us, and often reminds us that we aren't orphaned in our pigpens, we are sought by a Father whose arms long to embrace us. Paul expresses it this way, as a father speaking to his beloved children:

I do not write these things to make you ashamed,
>   but to admonish you as my beloved children.
>   For though you have countless guides in
>   Christ, you do not have many fathers. For I
>   became your father in Christ Jesus through
>   the gospel.
> *1 Corinthians 4:14–15*

I'm grateful for a great message that encourages and challenges us each week, but Jesus knew that discipleship required a much greater commitment to the growth of His children. And a father can say something to his kids that carries a far greater impact on his kids.

I'd love to end this chapter with, *and he lived happily ever after*, but our divorce in June of 2019 proved to merely be the gateway into my own personal wilderness. I'm better for it now, but it was bitter, and that bitterness was still very apparent well into 2021. You can't microwave the healing process. And yet, God's calling on my life hadn't been suspended or canceled.

I notified the church leadership that I was stepping away from being "pastor" to merely heal from our marriage of twenty-four years that had just ended. I would continue to lead, but less so as a pastor, and more so as just Mike. With their commitment to me, I took the better part of that first year to simply mourn the loss of my marriage.

The second year was more of a focus on who I am called to be in Christ, as opposed to what others expect of me as a "pastor." Both years were necessary.

·   ·   ·

Across the previous decade, I'd shelved many dreams God had given me, simply because it seemed purely selfish to consider writing a book, publishing a song, leading a mentoring program, etc., when my home was in jeopardy. *Why pick out curtains when there's a fire in the master bedroom? Why selfishly consider moving forward with any of these dreams when my marriage is in ICU?* And now, after failing in marriage:

Who wants a spiritually compromised (divorced) preacher spitting spiritual soliloquies? If he can't fix his own home, what good is his word anyway? I'm certain none of you reading this would have judged me so harshly (though some did), *but that's how I felt about me.*

So the dreams remained on the shelf into 2020 and 2021. What their shelf life was, I wasn't sure. Perhaps they'd never become reality. Yet, they remained intact... even in my darkness... even in my wilderness. I started dating in the summer of 2019, because the desire to have somebody beside me didn't merely dissipate.

This proved to be a landmine. I'm not saying that any of the women I'd seen were inherently evil or even bad. Each professed a love for Jesus, but my heart was off the table. I flirted, I kissed, I caressed, but my heart wasn't to be entrusted to anyone.

While I had betrayed my own marriage vows, I vowed to never let anyone have the kind of access to my heart that a rib has. A rib is meant to protect. A rib has too close of proximity to the heart, and this remains my greatest fear. *Why let anyone that close ever again?* For my part, my romantic endeavors were loveless. Most were innocent, and when a few of these ladies discerned everything but my heart was engaged, things would abruptly end. It didn't crush me, because I wouldn't willingly place myself in a position to become emotionally attached to anyone.

I had one long-term relationship, but I wasn't ready for that either. On a few occasions, I even admitted to my leadership team and our congregation that this relationship had gone off the rails. We'd crossed lines that I knew weren't pleasing to God, but the comfort of a woman was hard to simply walk away from. Even so, that kind of comfort would prove insufficient in the light of knowing I was still far from where God wanted me. By late 2020, I knew things needed to end, but even this didn't happen overnight. The process was enduring and the damage I inflicted was real. I'd hurt someone who deeply cared about me.

By 2021, I was finally starting to see daylight. The shackles I'd struggled to break free from in marriage no longer held me in their merciless grasp across two decades. I'd previously made choices that put me too close to the fire so as not to get burned. Yes, there were and remain holes in me, but I was navigating the waters more and more as a son. *Were there falls?* Yes. But less so than before. That October, I'd set a course to steer away from any of the landmines I'd previously ignored.

My heart was being restored to a firm place within God's purpose and design for me. *Am I cautious when it comes to dating?* Guarded like Fort Knox, I suppose, but my heart is no longer chained to sexual addiction or immorality. I am porn free. That chain broke in 2019. If I'm honest, and I hope there's some evidence of that by now, anything short of God's design for intimacy in marriage is a counterfeit, and a poor one at that.

I don't even think I ever wanted it for porn's sake but wanted everything anyone wants... a life partner... a friend and confidante, and yes, a lover... but porn was the empty substitute I'd retreated to in lieu of the real thing. I was lonely. I wanted the dream that was lost many years previously in our marriage.

Once I'd determined to return to the arms of my Father, the dreams slowly returned. I was still the son He'd asked to obey Him, though we both know I fail. I was still the son He'd anointed and called, and His calling is without repentance, even though it required deep repentance on my part.

I'm still the son He has purposed with dreams of writing books, a song and so much more...and I'm raising a group of leaders who I daily encourage to walk in a manner worthy of the Lord, yes, even while falling down at times. These young people have come so much further that I could've dreamed two years ago... even while I walked through my own valley of darkness... and they know I won't let go of them when they fall.

> We all like sheep have gone astray. Each of us
> has turned to his own way, yet the Lord has
> laid on Him the iniquity of us all.
> **Isaiah 53:6**

We don't have to pay the sin bill because it was paid on our behalf. The debt is no longer outstanding, so there's nothing standing in the way of our dreams that we once considered too far gone.

True restoration for prodigals requires the embrace of a father. Only then, did the kid in Luke 15 begin to dream the dream he'd once lost in his own lostness. When Dad embraced him, the heart became engaged again, and his dream of becoming everything Dad had ever dreamed of returned. Everything Dad had promised wasn't lost because Dad has his kid back in his arms. In His embrace, we are free to dream. I'm dreaming again like never before.

Hallelujah!

13

PLAYING FOR THE SECOND HALF

Aren't you glad that God doesn't feel about us the way we feel about us?

Our parents are buried next to each other in a graveyard in Lemmon, South Dakota. They celebrated their fiftieth anniversary on October first of 2000…Mom passed away less than two years later. Kevin and I had witnessed the financial struggles, the seasons of Dad's unemployment and the discouragement they persevered, all the while trying to keep that weight from weighing us down.

They weathered the storms of life together, amidst their own disappointments and yes, betrayals. Fifty-two years of togetherness…great highs and great lows. They set the bar very high for two boys whose identities were no longer Jimmy and Vickie's kids, or $600 commodities. We are their kids. We love Jesus and we play football.

In my mind, I'm *still* a quarterback and football is *still* my game. That's how Dad raised us. Sometimes I still think I'm a cowboy, but thus far…mostly just a couple hats and no cattle. At times I feel like a great lover, but yes, that will wait for now. Other times, I feel like a fighter who can still hold his own, provided the cause is just.

I'm a man who makes no apology for the way God created me. At times, this has conflicted with the role of pastor, and I'm okay with that. The past three years have been a renaissance and rediscovery for me.

That said, the greatest game I'd ever played in wasn't on the football field, but rather on a basketball court one spring morning in 1988. I was a freshman in high school… It was more than a game, it was one of the greatest life lessons God provided for this current season in my life, as I assess my life today and how much time is left on the clock. I turn fifty this year.

As a younger man, the clock didn't tick quite as loud as it does now. The score didn't seem to matter nearly as much, even when down by a considerable amount, because there was time. *The whole game is ahead of us when we're young, right?*

While I've never considered myself an elite basketball player, I was an athlete and the leading scorer on my freshman team out of Elgin, North Dakota. Because of my penchant to shoot, I quickly earned the nickname "John Wayne." I was pretty good...for a player on a small team in western North Dakota. That morning, we weren't playing on a traditional wood floor, but at an armory in Lemmon, South Dakota, with linoleum at our feet.

This flooring was the equivalent to the old-style turf on a football field... disaster for damaged knees. It was the first quarter and I jumped to rebound a missed shot from a teammate, and upon landing, felt my ACL tear, sending me to the floor. Everyone within proximity said they'd heard the pop, and I let out an agonizing yell as I hit the opaque flooring beneath me. As a fourteen-year-old, the pain was excruciating, and I knew this was far more serious than I cared to let on.

Immediately I pulled myself to my feet and tested my weight on my left knee. It wasn't holding. It was the first of eight complete ACL tears that led to surgery and extensive physical therapy.

I was injured beyond any thought of returning to the game... after all, *it was just basketball*. Football was my first love in sports. As I sat out the remainder of the first quarter and the entirety of the second quarter...something I wasn't used to doing...I was tortured by the throbbing in my left knee and by our diminishing prospect of winning this tournament.

Until I was injured, we'd remained competitive against our opponent, maintaining a slight lead. When I left the court, our lead soon dwindled to a ten-point deficit...then twenty...all the way to twenty-six points.

At during the second quarter, I did something unusual. Oklahoma Sooner legend and Seattle Seahawk linebacker Brian Bosworth was a personal (football) hero for my brother and me in our high school years. His *Land of Boz* poster hung on Kevin's bedroom wall, while the mullet and shaved sides Brian sported in pics were fashioned into Kevin's own hairstyle. Our parents hated it. I didn't go as far as shaving my own head, but I remember sporting a shirt he promoted: *Real Men Wear Black.* Still wish I had it...but in a slightly larger size now. In the center of his book, there were five to seven pages of pictures, one of which presented Brian completely naked on a folding chair while taking a shower.

I was angry, and what better way to express my own outrage at my current dilemma than emulating my angry hero? I disrobed, grabbed a chair, and got under the water. *Makes perfect sense, right?* Stay with me. (Sidenote: In May of 2012, I officiated Brian Bosworth's wedding to his beautiful wife in Dallas, Texas. For the record, nobody was naked that afternoon.)

Under the cold water of that shower, I determined that I'd man up, feign an earlier overreaction, and request my return to the court. After a little coaxing, our coach agreed to test this out. After all, we were down by twenty-six points...*there's nothing to lose*, he reasoned. Inwardly grimacing with every step, I conspicuously hobbled onto the floor and felt *I had nothing to lose either.*

I played no defense that half; instead, I opted to play between the three-point lines on either side. As the scoring leader on our team, perhaps my presence alone encouraged our team, but when I began to shoot the ball, I wasn't missing...so I kept shooting. Here and there one of my teammates would secure a rebound, find the net, and we began to rally. I simply shot the ball and watched my team's four-man defense defend against their five-man offense.

Our group would get a rebound, get me the ball and I'd shoot. We were all aware that the clock didn't favor our victory...we were under a seemingly insurmountable point deficiency. The clock ticked very loudly...only louder was the unbearable pain emanating from my left knee. I'd played hurt before, but never with such an enduring (and career-threatening) injury.

When the final buzzer sounded, we'd won the game and I had set a personal single game scoring record for myself, all from three-point territory. If I'm honest, that was the least I took away from the game that day.

Winning always feels good...especially to competitor types, like myself. However, the bigger win came from recognizing that to succeed, you cannot give up, just because the clock says your defeat is imminent and the scoreboard is mercilessly taunting you. I brought something back onto the court for the second half greater than my athleticism or my basketball prowess...it was an unwillingness to just sit there and do nothing with the time I had left on the clock, even injured as I was.

For many my age, including myself (at times), we've concluded that we've wasted so much of the clock, and that life has brought us to a place of such injury, whether from a divorce, a betrayal, addiction, a death of a spouse or child, or whatever… with everything against us at this point, victory isn't even worth considering anymore. The clock ticks too loudly.

The scoreboard is too weighted against us. The opponent needn't yell at all…*we tell ourselves it's over…we tell ourselves we're too far gone…we tell ourselves that we can never again return to the place where our dreams once lived. We reckon God is mad and rightly disappointed…and we are no longer worthy to be called sons or daughters of the Most High. Aren't you glad that God doesn't feel about us the way we feel about us?*

My encouragement to you, after rereading Luke 15…is to get naked, grab a folding chair and a cold shower, and determine to get back out there and play like you've never played before… deeply injured…emotionally tormented…against all odds…with whatever time remains. Shoot wildly and celebrate when the first bucket hits. With every missed shot…let it go…we've had a lifetime of those missed shots and that didn't kill or retire us… get the ball back and go for it. Others have taken their comfy place on the bench for much less…you're still in the game. You're hurt…you're not dead.

The odds were against Abraham, David, Moses, Joshua, Mary (Jesus' mother), Daniel, the Three Hebrew Boys, Elijah, Mary Magdalene, Samson, Esther…*you get the picture.* You can bring something far greater to the table than your talent and experience…it's the ability to still believe when others around you cannot see any reason to keep believing…but they cannot help but see your faith in those moments.

This is what leaders do. It's the determination to bind ourselves to our convictions rather than our conditions. If our conditions are determinative, we will constantly be tossed by every wind and wave that comes along and paralyzes others. If our convictions are determinative, we've found a good enough hill to die on *and die we may…* but we'll have done so for reasons worthy of our sacrifice.

For whatever reason, Mom and Dad weren't there that day to see my best game ever. They rarely missed any of our games. The two people who were always there when needed the most, didn't see my fall that day. They weren't present to witness my comeback. They'd only hear about it later with joy.

Ironically, in a graveyard less than a mile from where I fell that day, and later rose to victory, Mom and Dad are buried next to each other. This was by God's design. In the place where my own fears of losing a game gripped me so severely, I stood watch as my parents' caskets were lowered into the ground, and I considered how I would recover from their absence. *How do I face the last half of my life without them? This new limp wouldn't disappear with a little rest and physical therapy. I've got the second half of my life to play the game, and they won't be here.*

At forty-nine, I've got less time on the clock, and at times, I feel like the injuries I've acquired and self-inflicted are too much to overcome. That's not faith talking, just my feelings at times. Feelings are real but shouldn't be trusted. Faith tells me that, severe as my injuries may be, I've played on this treacherous linoleum before, and despite the deficit…and the clock…and the injury…no victory comes from sitting it out, but with grueling endurance and faith in what I couldn't imagine for the result. I've been here before, I'm about to start shooting again despite any of those factors. I hope you will too.

Let's not end with basketball. My heart won't let me…I tore my ACL seven times for football and only once for basketball. I'm completely biased toward pigskin. Once more, I will speak of the impact a father can have on a son. Let's talk in football terms. My brother Kevin and I will attest, Dad and Mom rarely missed a game of ours.

When Dad wasn't filming and Mom wasn't screaming next to him, Dad would meander down to the sidelines where he could talk to Kevin and me. In our high school years, he was already in his sixties, but for his two boys, his presence on the field outweighed a thousand people in the stands…even the coaches.

On offense, Kevin was usually a fullback and I played quarterback. We were always in sync together on offense from years of throwing the ball in the yard, night after night, with Dad. But it was on defense that Dad's presence was acutely felt. Kevin knows this. (Kevin spent most of his time on defense as a linebacker, while I played free safety).

On the sideline, you could always spot Dad with his fedora and overcoat…and more than likely, taking a swig from what I'd guess was a pretty lame cup of coffee. *But he was right there*. He never knew this, but I would whisper or silently offer a response every time I heard him say two words. In those two

words, he was telling us that he *saw us*…that he was *with us*…
that he *knew we could handle what was coming*…and he was
calling us by name…his own name. *Those two words?*

"*C'mon Ryherd!*"

Those *two words* will never leave me. Upon hearing those
two words, as a free safety, I didn't care what or who or how
(big) was coming through the line of scrimmage, my objective,
because Dad was watching…was to hit whoever was carrying
the ball with every ounce of my being *simply because* he was
watching and that's how he'd raised us. There was no way I'd
be the one to cower…Dad would see it. That's not us.

Yes, I'm still probably limping a little more than I care to
admit. Yes, there is less time on the clock than I had twenty
years ago. And yes, at this point, there are parts of life where
winning seems impossible. However, there *remains* some time
on the clock to *swing for the fence* to mix our metaphors up a
bit. There *remains* the knowledge that Kevin and I shouldn't
have gotten this far… but for God's mercy. And there's *still the
memory* of a mom who wouldn't stop cheering for us with her
every breath and a dad who was proudly watching us as he
called us his own… all from a $600 investment one day in 1973.

(*Hey Kevin, we've got to make good on this.*)

Behind my facemask and under my breath, as aware of his
presence on the sidelines as he was of my place on the football
field, my response to Dad's words was always the same as I
braced for what was just ahead:

"*Dad…watch this!*"

14

FINDING OUR WAY HOME

Home is embracing the dreams I'd almost lost...now being fully convinced that they were never lost...I was.

I don't remember the trauma or neglect that was the first chapter of Kevin's and my life…*but it's my story…our story…shared by twelve of us.* I was certain I wouldn't be the sibling penning anything autobiographical, because for the last forty-nine years, I'd distanced myself from anything called family that didn't look like the family I grew up with. For me, to truly embrace this story, felt like a bad relapse. *Who wants to fight to get clean from the needle simply to relapse? Who wants to remember life before hope? Who wants to return to the house that felt like anything but home?*

In July of 2021, while I was spending some time alone with God, He encouraged me to write. In my mind, *I was a pastor whose fall was too recent. A divorcé who'd compromised his own home. A father who was angry that he hadn't done better. Mostly, I felt like a son who was too far from home to consider a return.*

"Whether you write or not, this is **My story** *and the mess I rescued you from."*

"It's one thing to consider writing about our first chapter and the mess (no fault of our own) that we were born into. I'm not nearly as comfortable writing about the mess I've made for myself and others since that time." I internally contested for about two months in prayer.

"I rescued you then and I'll do it again. Even now, as injured, and unqualified as you might feel at times, there are others who feel that way in life, and your life is a testimony to what I can do."

> But **now**, thus says the Lord, your Creator, O
> Jacob, and He who formed you, O Israel, "Do
> not fear, for I have redeemed you; I have
> called you by name; you are Mine!"
> **Isaiah 43:1**

As a believer, it's so much easier to believe for the prodigal kid in Luke 15, than for ourselves when we've blown it…when the dream seems irreconcilable with our future and its fulfillment. Nonetheless, that story was never written for that kid, *his story was written for us…at times when we need the reminder the most.* The dream isn't lost because we've fallen… and stop believing in ourselves…but when we stop believing in the One who, knowing every painful chapter and verse, promised to be faithful through it all.

He is the Author and Finisher of those who place their faith in Him…meaning He who began this work in you and me isn't settled on the last chapter as the tragic ending, but as an opportunity for Him to be the hero once again. In Hebrew, He is *Yehoshua*…i.e., *the God who saves*. In English, His name is *Jesus*. Like me, if you recall the stories in the Gospels, there isn't a single instance where He wasn't willing to save the broken or sinful individuals He encountered, only those who refused to place their faith in Him to do so.

If you're a mess, the good news is that Jesus is in the business of saving addicts, divorcé, the sexually immoral, the idolatrous, the lost…but the bad news is that many attempt to navigate their comeback without Him. He's the *only* way home.

> Salvation is found in no one else; for there is no
> other name given under heaven by which we
> must be saved.
> *Acts 4:12*

Mom and Dad didn't fail in raising us boys, we just got ourselves a little lost along the way at times. They knew we'd need to know the way home at such times, and they gave us an example each day of Who to run to when we did.

Failure as a parent isn't making mistakes or sinning, but sweeping things under the rug so meticulously, that in our failure, they don't see in us a pattern of repentance and trust in our Father to be loving enough to forgive and restore us…and in turn, for them (our kids) when they will need it most.

So what does finding home feel like as I write this final chapter?

There's still some transition and a lot of unlearning for me to do. God's love and mercy isn't a theological proposition for me to merely preach or studiously extrapolate; it's oxygen to my lungs. It's the reason to keep going when home seems lost… *God didn't run from prostitutes… God didn't run from evil… God never ran from a fight… "The only time I ever saw Him run was when He ran to me"… He runs to embrace us.*

Home is a hug or a "Dad, I love you" from my daughters. *Is there collateral damage from years of sweeping things under the rug?* Yes, but the God who rescued me is the One who loves my girls far more than I ever could and has paid a far greater price for each of them, than I have.

. . .

Yes, my tattooed forearm bears their names and the axiom that for those three, "*I could die smiling,*"; and if it came to it, I'd make good on it with a smile. *That's exactly what Jesus did.* The marks on His own body are the proof. He agonized more at the thought of losing one of His kids than at His own death. The thought of us responding to His offer brings heaven a smile every time.

Home is a long conversation with my brother Kevin and his wife, Jennifer, who through my mess have been there for me in a way that would make Mom and Dad so proud. It's laughing out loud over things Mom would chastise us both for, whereupon Dad would attempt to calm her down a little, assuring her we are just joking around.

It's reflecting on our childhood misadventures… past girlfriends, memories on the football field together… mutual friends we stay in contact with… and now, a lot of conversation about the gravity of what we came through to get here.

Home is any opportunity to sit with Larry Titus for a pancake or any other reason… even for bad reasons or contrived ones. He is the father who embraced me when I felt unlovable and unworthy. After my dad's passing, he is the father figure in my life who I felt like I'd disappointed the most, and the same man who God used to restore me the most.

I'm convinced, and hope to convince you, that while a pastor or preacher has his place, it'll never replace having a father (1 Corinthians 4:15) constantly speak over us… in the pigpens we find ourselves in…speaking what only a dad can speak. *This is discipleship and it's hard to find.*

. . .

Home is the routine trip to Carlsbad, New Mexico, to visit one of our ministry's elders, Bill Bower, who remains one of the greatest blessings to me personally, and to our ministry. He is partly to blame for me remaining in ministry when I was ready to hang up my jersey for good.

As I approach midfield in terms of years (I turn fifty in December of 2022), home is the opportunity to engage with new brothers and sisters in their thirties and forties…some of whom I've still never met. Our story is being turned into a television show this year. As the documentary progresses, we're going to be spending some time together on set and off.

I suspect seeing all the siblings together will have the awkwardness of a first date once again, but it will also give us an opportunity to not only learn about the past chapters that can't be unwritten, but to create some new ones together. I have no idea about the dynamics of having the twelve of us together in one room. *Who are the extroverts and who are the introverts? Who will be the most dramatic? The mouthiest? The funniest? Most annoying? What about this story will be uncovered in the light of the camera?* Stay tuned.

Home is a call from one of my high school and college friends, or those who stuck it out with me through my wilderness time… and some new friends that I've met since then.

It's the family of believers of Kingdom Echo Ministries in Denton, Texas, who, in their own messes, patiently allowed me to walk through my brokenness without judgment or condemnation…and yes, even through failures. My Church has never felt more like family than it does now.

They are the disciples I am most proud of across years of ministry. Those who've been with me across the last two years are transparent to a fault and loved far more than I can express. I'm way more excited about them and their potential than they are, but I forgive them. Discipleship works and they are my evidence. I'm 100 percent committed to each of them.

It's an open Bible in one hand, and at times, a cigar in the other on an open-air patio. It's time alone with God where it doesn't seem nearly as much like forced prayer, but "Father-son" time where we just hang out with no expectations and talk...*together* is the goal. Home is embracing the dreams I'd almost lost, i.e., given up on...though I now understand more clearly, the dreams were never lost...I was (for a time).

If I'm honest, home is considering that God has the right "one" still out there for me. One who won't mind getting kicked out of a few spots with me ...my ride or die. Someone to share the dream with...to minister with...to pick on a little...to pick on a lot...to laugh and cry with...to dance with...someone who I'd rather argue with than not argue without...someone to write the remaining chapters with.

Larry, who I affectionately call "Dad" because he is my father in the faith (and because I consider myself his favorite son), recently challenged me: "*Mike, keep your fingerprints off the next one, and let God put His fingerprints all over the next marriage relationship He has for you.*" *Pretty good Dad advice, right?*

In his last Christmas letter to Kevin and me, our adoptive father, Ellis Ryherd, wrote one line. His wife, who he'd married a few years after our mom's passing, had written the entirety of the letter, but for the end. Dad's line: *Jesus is more than the reason for the season. Jesus is the everything of Christmas. He's the Everything of everything. Merry Christmas!* If you ever get a Christmas card from me, *and I don't write Christmas cards…* I'm sure I won't write much beyond that, but that's what you'd read from me if I did.

Mom and Dad, Kevin and I love you, and in heaven's timing, we will see you again. But until then, "Watch this!"

I'm going to leave you with a short story about finding home. For those who believe they've strayed further than the grace of God can reach, please listen to the following with your heart, because it's God's heart toward each one of us.

A man was seated comfortably in his recliner one evening reading the morning newspaper that had been delivered earlier that day. As he read, his attention ventured out his living room window toward a small figure on the curb where he'd just fetched his paper. There he saw a little girl, maybe four or five years old, sobbing. He immediately got up from his chair and went to see about her.
"Little girl, why are you crying?"
"Because I followed a dog and now I'm lost. I don't know where my house is," she exclaimed between sobs.
The man proceeded to ask a few questions in the hopes of getting her home.

"Do you know where you live?" he inquired softly.

"Yes…I live at my house" she breathed out between muffled cries.

He smiled and tried again.

"Do you know your mom's name?" he continued.

She nodded affirmatively.

"Mommy," she whispered

Hearing her *name* only brought on more tears.

The man would try yet again.

"Do you remember anything about your house? What street do you live on? Is it near a school or a park where you play?

At this, the little girl, wiping her tears, looked up with some hope in her eyes and confidently expressed:

*"My dad will often push me in the swing in our backyard, and when I swing really high, I can see over our fence. There's a church next to our house with a large white cross on top. **Mister, if you can get me to that cross, I can find my way home."***

ABOUT THE AUTHOR

Mike is senior leader of Kingdom Echo Ministries in Denton, Texas. Discipleship is at the heart of everything he is called to, which includes a weekly podcast, developing leaders through discipleship intensives, writing and more.
Visit mikeryherd.com for more information.

Made in the USA
Monee, IL
12 August 2023